# ultimate
# party food
## book

Publications International, Ltd.

Favorite Brand Name Recipes at www.fbnr.com

**Pictured on the front cover:** Blue Crab Stuffed Tomatoes *(page 16).*

**Pictured on the front jacket flap:** Tipsy Chicken Wraps *(page 18).*

**Pictured on the back cover:** Ham & Cheese Quesadillas with Cherry Jam *(page 10).*

ISBN-13: 978-1-4127-2669-6
ISBN-10: 1-4127-2669-7

Library of Congress Control Number: 2007932083

Manufactured in China.

8 7 6 5 4 3 2 1

**Microwave Cooking:** Microwave ovens vary in wattage. Use the cooking times as guidelines and check for doneness before adding more time.

**Preparation/Cooking Times:** Preparation times are based on the approximate amount of time required to assemble the recipe before cooking, baking, chilling or serving. These times include preparation steps such as measuring, chopping and mixing. The fact that some preparations and cooking can be done simultaneously is taken into account. Preparation of optional ingredients and serving suggestions is not included.

# Table of Contents

# Party starters

# Chicken Satay Skewers

6 garlic cloves, chopped
4 teaspoons dried coriander
4 teaspoons light brown sugar
2 teaspoons salt
$1\frac{1}{2}$ teaspoons HERSHEY®S Cocoa
1 teaspoon ground black pepper
$\frac{1}{2}$ cup soy sauce
6 tablespoons vegetable oil
2 tablespoons lime juice
4 teaspoons fresh chopped ginger
$2\frac{1}{2}$ pounds boneless, skinless chicken breasts
Peanut Dipping Sauce (recipe follows)
$\frac{1}{4}$ cup fresh cilantro, chopped (optional)

1. Combine garlic, coriander, brown sugar, salt, cocoa and pepper in large bowl. Stir in soy sauce, oil, lime juice and ginger.

2. Cut chicken into $1\frac{1}{2}$- to 2-inch cubes. Add to soy sauce mixture, stirring to coat chicken pieces. Cover; marinate in refrigerator for at least 2 hours.

3. Meanwhile, prepare Peanut Dipping Sauce. Thread chicken pieces onto skewers. Grill or broil, basting with marinade. Discard leftover marinade. Garnish with chopped cilantro, if desired. Serve with peanut sauce. Refrigerate leftovers. *Makes 15 to 20 appetizers*

## Peanut Dipping Sauce

$\frac{1}{2}$ cup peanut oil
1 cup REESE'S® Crunchy Peanut Butter
$\frac{1}{4}$ cup lime juice
$\frac{1}{4}$ cup soy sauce
3 tablespoons honey
2 garlic cloves, minced
1 teaspoon cayenne pepper
$\frac{1}{2}$ teaspoon hot pepper sauce

Gradually whisk peanut oil into peanut butter in medium bowl. Blend in lime juice, soy sauce, honey, garlic, cayenne pepper and hot pepper sauce. Adjust flavors to taste for a sweet/hot flavor.        *Makes 2$\frac{1}{4}$ cups*

## Brie Bites

1 package (17$\frac{1}{2}$ ounces) frozen puff pastry sheets, thawed
$\frac{1}{4}$ cup apricot preserves or red pepper jelly
1 (5-inch) brie round, cut into 32 chunks

1. Preheat oven to 400°F. Cut each puff pastry sheet into 16 squares.

2. Spread $\frac{1}{2}$ teaspoon apricot preserves on each square. Place one cube of brie on one side of each square. Fold over opposite edge; use tines of fork to seal completely. Place 1 inch apart on ungreased baking sheets.

3. Bake 10 to 13 minutes or until pastry is golden brown.

*Makes 32 bites*

# Apple Salsa with Cilantro and Lime

1 cup diced unpeeled red apples
$^1/_4$ cup diced red onion
$^1/_4$ cup minced Anaheim chile pepper
$^1/_2$ jalapeño pepper, seeded and minced* (optional)
2 tablespoons lime juice
1 teaspoon chopped fresh cilantro
$^1/_4$ teaspoon black pepper
$^1/_8$ teaspoon salt
Tortilla chips

*Jalapeño peppers can sting and irritate the skin, so wear rubber gloves when handling peppers and do not touch your eyes.

1. Combine apples, onion, chile pepper, jalapeño pepper, if desired, lime juice, cilantro, black pepper and salt in large bowl; mix well. Cover with plastic wrap and refrigerate at least 30 minutes or overnight.

2. Serve with tortilla chips.

*Makes 2 cups*

Anaheim chile peppers or California green chiles are light green with a mild flavor and a slight bite. If you prefer a hotter salsa, add the green jalapeño pepper to the recipe. For a sweeter salsa, add a red jalapeño pepper.

# Ham & Cheese Quesadillas with Cherry Jam

1 tablespoon vegetable oil
1 cup thinly sliced red onion
1 small jalapeño pepper, seeded and minced*
1 cup pitted fresh sweet cherries
1 tablespoon packed brown sugar
1 teaspoon balsamic vinegar
$\frac{1}{4}$ teaspoon salt
2 (9-inch) flour tortillas
3 ounces ham, thinly sliced
2 ounces Havarti cheese, thinly sliced
2 teaspoons butter

*Jalapeño peppers can sting and irritate the skin, so wear rubber gloves when handling peppers and do not touch your eyes.*

1. Heat oil in large skillet over medium-high heat. Add onion and jalapeño pepper; cook and stir 3 minutes or until onions are golden. Add cherries; cook and stir 1 minute. Stir in brown sugar, vinegar and salt. Cook over low heat 1 minute, stirring constantly. Remove from heat; cool slightly.

2. Arrange half of ham slices and half of cheese slices over one side of each tortilla. Top with one fourth of cherry jam. Fold tortillas in half. Remove and reserve any remaining jam.

3. Wipe out skillet. Melt butter in skillet over medium heat. Add quesadillas; press down firmly with spatula. Cook 3 to 4 minutes per side or until golden and cheese melts. Remove from skillet. Cut each quesadilla in half. Serve with remaining cherry jam.                    *Makes 2 servings*

# Cool Shrimp Spring Rolls with
## Wasabi Soy Dipping Sauce

1 cup *French's® Gourmayo™* Wasabi Horseradish Light Mayonnaise
2 tablespoons soy sauce
2 tablespoons lemon juice
1 tablespoon grated peeled fresh ginger
1 tablespoon minced green onion
4 cups shredded cabbage mix
12 (9-inch) rice paper wrappers, soaked in cold water until softened
36 shelled cooked medium shrimp (about $\frac{1}{2}$ pound)
6 cups shredded Iceberg or Romaine lettuce

1. Prepare Wasabi Soy Dipping Sauce: Combine mayonnaise, soy sauce, lemon juice, ginger and green onion in measuring cup. Pour $\frac{3}{4}$ cup sauce into medium bowl; add cabbage and toss to combine. Cover and chill remaining sauce.

2. Place 1 rice paper wrapper on work surface. Arrange 3 shrimp across center of wrapper. Top with about 2 tablespoons cabbage mixture and $\frac{1}{2}$ cup shredded lettuce. Fold sides of wrapper in, then roll up. Repeat with remaining wrappers and ingredients.

3. To serve: Arrange 2 spring rolls on serving plate. Garnish with peanuts and green onions, if desired. Serve with remaining Wasabi Soy Dipping Sauce.                                              *Makes 6 servings*

Note: Rice paper wrappers are available in Asian grocery markets and gourmet specialty stores.

Prep Time: 30 minutes

# Falafel Nuggets

2 cans (15 ounces each) chickpeas
$\frac{1}{2}$ cup whole wheat flour
$\frac{1}{2}$ cup chopped fresh parsley
$\frac{1}{3}$ cup lemon juice
$\frac{1}{4}$ cup minced onion
2 tablespoons minced garlic
2 teaspoons ground cumin
$\frac{1}{2}$ teaspoon salt
$\frac{1}{2}$ teaspoon ground red pepper or red pepper flakes
$\frac{1}{2}$ cup canola oil

Sauce

$2\frac{1}{2}$ cups tomato sauce
$\frac{1}{3}$ cup tomato paste
2 tablespoons lemon juice
2 teaspoons sugar
1 teaspoon dry onion powder
$\frac{1}{2}$ teaspoon salt

1. Preheat oven to 400°F. Coat baking sheet with nonstick cooking spray.

2. For falafel, drain chickpeas, reserving $\frac{1}{4}$ cup liquid. Combine chickpeas, reserved liquid, flour, parsley, $\frac{1}{3}$ cup lemon juice, minced onion, garlic, cumin, $\frac{1}{2}$ teaspoon salt and red pepper in food processor or blender; cover and process until well blended. Shape mixture into 36 (1-inch) balls; place 1 to 2 inches apart on baking sheet. Refrigerate 15 minutes.

3. Heat oil in large nonstick skillet over medium-high heat. Fry falafel in batches until browned. Place on baking sheet; bake 8 to 10 minutes.

4. For sauce, combine tomato sauce, tomato paste, 2 tablespoons lemon juice, sugar, onion powder and $\frac{1}{2}$ teaspoon salt in medium saucepan. Simmer over medium-low heat 20 minutes. Serve with falafel.

*Makes 12 servings*

# Beef and Lettuce Bundles

1 pound ground beef
$\frac{1}{2}$ cup sliced green onions
1 clove garlic, minced
$\frac{2}{3}$ cup chopped water chestnuts
$\frac{1}{2}$ cup chopped red bell pepper
1 tablespoon soy sauce
1 tablespoon seasoned rice vinegar
2 tablespoons chopped fresh cilantro
1 or 2 heads leaf lettuce, separated into leaves (discard outer leaves)
Hoisin sauce (optional)

1. Brown beef 6 to 8 minutes in large skillet over medium-high heat, stirring to break up meat. Drain fat. Add green onions and garlic. Cook until tender. Stir in water chestnuts, bell pepper, soy sauce and vinegar. Cook until bell pepper is crisp-tender and most of liquid has evaporated, stirring occasionally.

2. Stir in cilantro. Spoon meat mixture onto lettuce leaves; sprinkle with hoisin sauce, if desired. Wrap lettuce leaves around meat mixture to make bundles.

*Makes 8 servings*

Party Starters

# Blue Crab Stuffed Tomatoes

$^1/_2$ pound Florida blue crabmeat
10 plum tomatoes
$^1/_2$ cup finely chopped celery
$^1/_3$ cup plain yogurt
 2 tablespoons minced green onion
 2 tablespoons finely chopped red bell pepper
$^1/_2$ teaspoon lemon juice
$^1/_4$ teaspoon salt
$^1/_8$ teaspoon black pepper

Remove any shell or cartilage from crabmeat.

Cut tomatoes in half lengthwise. Carefully scoop out centers of tomatoes; discard pulp. Invert on paper towels.

Combine crabmeat, celery, yogurt, onion, red pepper, lemon juice, salt and black pepper. Mix well.

Fill tomato halves with crab mixture. Refrigerate 2 hours.

*Makes 20 appetizers*

Favorite recipe from Florida Department of Agriculture and Consumer Services, Bureau of Seafood and Aquaculture

# Tipsy Chicken Wraps

1 tablespoon sesame oil
1 pound ground chicken
8 ounces firm tofu, diced
3 green onions, sliced
2 cloves garlic, minced
$\frac{1}{2}$ red bell pepper, diced
1 tablespoon minced fresh ginger
$\frac{1}{2}$ cup Asian beer
$\frac{1}{3}$ cup hoisin sauce
1 teaspoon hot chile paste
$\frac{1}{2}$ cup chopped peanuts
2 heads Boston lettuce, cored, washed and
    separated into large leaves
Whole fresh chives

1. Heat oil over medium heat in large skillet. Brown chicken 6 to 8 minutes, stirring to break up meat. Remove from heat and drain in colander to remove excess liquid. Return to pan. Add tofu, green onions, garlic, bell pepper and ginger to skillet; cook until onions are softened. Add beer, hoisin sauce and chile paste; cook until heated through. Stir in chopped peanuts.

2. Place spoonful of chicken mixture in center of each lettuce leaf, edges curling upward. Fold up burrito-style. Wrap chives around filled leaves and tie to secure. *Makes about 20 wraps*

# Chili Puffs

1 package (about 17 ounces) frozen puff pastry sheets, thawed
1 can (15 ounces) chili without beans
$\frac{1}{2}$ package (4 ounces) cream cheese, softened
$\frac{1}{2}$ cup (2 ounces) finely shredded sharp Cheddar cheese
   Sliced green onion (optional)

1. Preheat oven to 400°F.

2. Roll each sheet of puff pastry into 18×9-inch rectangle on lightly floured surface. Cut each rectangle into 18 (3-inch) squares. Press dough into 36 mini (1$\frac{3}{4}$-inch) muffin cups. Bake 10 minutes.

3. Combine chili and cream cheese in medium bowl until smooth. Fill each pastry shell with 2 teaspoons chili mixture, pressing down centers of pastry to fill, if necessary. Sprinkle evenly with cheese.

4. Bake 5 to 7 minutes or until cheese is melted and edges of pastry are golden brown. Let stand in pan 5 minutes. Remove from pan. Garnish with green onion. *Makes 36 puffs*

*tip*

Puff pastry is a rich but delicate and flaky multi-layered pastry. It is prepared by repeatedly layering thin sheets of pastry dough with bits of butter and rolling and folding. When baked, the moisture in the melting butter creates steam, causing the pastry to puff and separate into crispy layers.

# Mexican Roll-Ups

2 packages (3 ounces each) cream cheese, softened
$^3/_4$ cup sour cream
1 package (15.2 ounces) ORTEGA® Soft Taco Kit
1 can (4 ounces) ORTEGA Diced Green Chiles, drained
$^3/_4$ cup finely shredded Cheddar cheese
20 ($2^1/_2 \times {}^3/_8$-inch) roasted red pepper strips

**BEAT** together cream cheese, sour cream and seasoning mix from Soft Taco Kit until smooth. Stir in green chiles and Cheddar cheese.

**SPREAD** 3 tablespoons cream cheese mixture evenly over each tortilla from kit. Place 2 red pepper strips in center of each tortilla; roll up and wrap in plastic wrap.

**CHILL** at least 3 hours.

**CUT** each roll-up into 7 ($^3/_4$-inch) slices.

**SERVE** with taco sauce from kit for dipping.          *Makes 70 roll-ups*

Note: Roasted red pepper strips can be purchased in 16-ounce jars in the condiment section at most supermarkets.

# Ranch Style Shrimp and Bacon Appetizers

**Ranch Style Barbecue Sauce (recipe follows)**
**30 large peeled, deveined shrimp**
**$^1/_2$ pound thick-cut bacon**
**10 wooden skewers***

*\*To prevent wooden skewers from burning while grilling or broiling, soak in water about 10 minutes before using.*

1. Prepare Ranch Style Barbecue Sauce.

2. Wrap each shrimp with $^1/_2$ bacon strip. Thread 3 wrapped shrimp onto each wooden skewer.

3. Grill or broil shrimp skewers until bacon is cooked and shrimp is no longer translucent, but has turned pink. Baste with barbecue sauce. Return to heat to warm sauce. Serve with additional barbecue sauce, if desired.

*Makes 10 shrimp skewers*

## Ranch Style Barbecue Sauce

**$^1/_4$ cup vegetable or olive oil**
**$^1/_2$ cup minced onion**
**2 garlic cloves, minced**
**2 tablespoons lemon juice**
**1 tablespoon ground black pepper**
**1 teaspoon *each* dry mustard and paprika**
**$^1/_2$ teaspoon *each* salt and hot pepper sauce**
**1$^1/_2$ cups ketchup**
**1 cup HEATH® BITS 'O BRICKLE™ Toffee Bits**
**$^1/_4$ cup cider vinegar**
**3 tablespoons sugar**
**1$^1/_2$ tablespoons HERSHEY'S Cocoa**

1. Heat oil in large saucepan over medium heat; add onion and garlic. Cook until tender. Stir in lemon juice, black pepper, mustard, paprika, salt and hot pepper sauce. Simmer for 5 minutes; reduce heat.

2. Stir in ketchup, toffee bits, vinegar, sugar and cocoa. Simmer 15 minutes. Refrigerate leftovers. *Makes 3 cups*

# Beef & Roasted Pepper Crostini

$3/4$ **pound thinly sliced deli roast beef**
**3 tablespoons olive oil**
**2 large cloves garlic, crushed**
**2 loaves (8 ounces each) French bread (about $2^1/2$-inch diameter), cut into $^1/2$-inch-thick slices**
**1 jar (12 ounces) roasted red peppers, rinsed, drained, chopped**
**2 cups shredded Italian cheese blend**

1. Heat oven to 450°F. In 1-cup glass measure, combine oil and garlic; microwave on HIGH 30 seconds. Lightly brush top side of each bread slice with oil mixture; arrange on 2 baking sheets. Bake in 450°F oven 6 to 8 minutes or until light golden brown.

2. Layer equal amounts of beef, red peppers and cheese over toasted bread. Return to oven; bake additional 2 to 4 minutes or until cheese is melted. Serve immediately. *Makes about 36 appetizers*

Tip: Bread may be toasted ahead of time and stored in airtight container.

Prep and Cook Time: 30 minutes

Favorite recipe from **National Cattlemen's Beef Association on Behalf of The Beef Checkoff**

# Sweet & Spicy Beer Nuts

**2 cups pecan halves**
**2 teaspoons chili powder**
**$^1/_2$ teaspoon ground cumin**
**$^1/_4$ teaspoon ground red pepper**
**2 teaspoons salt**
**2 teaspoons olive oil**
**$^1/_2$ cup sugar**
**$^1/_2$ cup beer**

1. Preheat oven to 350°F. Line baking sheet with foil.

2. Mix pecans, chili powder, cumin, red pepper, salt and olive oil in small bowl. Spread onto prepared baking sheet. Toast 10 minutes or until fragrant. Cool on baking sheet on wire rack.

3. Combine sugar and beer in small saucepan. Heat to 250°F, using candy thermometer. Remove from heat; carefully stir in nuts and any loose spices. Spread sugared nuts on baking sheet, separating clusters with wooden spoon.

4. Let cool completely. Break up any large pieces and serve in small dish.

*Makes 3 cups*

# French-Style Pizza Bites

2 tablespoons olive oil
1 medium onion, thinly sliced
1 medium red bell pepper, cut into 3-inch-long strips
2 cloves garlic, minced
$\frac{1}{3}$ cup pitted black olives, cut into thin wedges
1 can (10 ounces) refrigerated pizza crust dough
$\frac{3}{4}$ cup (3 ounces) finely shredded Swiss or Gruyère cheese

1. Position oven rack to lowest position. Preheat oven to 425°F.

2. Heat oil in medium skillet over medium heat. Add onion, bell pepper and garlic. Cook and stir 5 minutes or until crisp-tender. Stir in olives. Remove from heat; set aside.

3. Pat dough into 16×12-inch rectangle on large greased cookie sheet. Arrange onion mixture over dough. Sprinkle with cheese. Bake 10 minutes. Loosen crust with long spatula; slide onto oven rack. Bake 3 to 5 minutes more or until golden brown.

4. Slide cookie sheet under crust and remove crust from rack. Transfer to cutting board. Cut dough crosswise into eight 1$\frac{3}{4}$-inch-wide strips. Cut dough diagonally into ten 2-inch-wide strips, making diamond pieces. Serve immediately. *Makes about 24 servings*

# Creamy Mushroom Cups

2 tablespoons butter

4 ounces mushrooms, coarsely chopped

$1/4$ teaspoon salt

2 cloves garlic, minced

2 tablespoons dry sherry

$1/4$ cup whipping cream

15 frozen phyllo shells, thawed and warmed

$1/4$ cup chopped fresh parsley

1. Melt butter in large nonstick skillet over medium heat. Add mushrooms and salt; cook 3 minutes or until tender, stirring frequently. Add garlic; cook and stir 15 seconds.

2. Add sherry; stir to blend. Stir in cream; cook and stir 2 minutes or until thickened.

3. Divide mushroom mixture evenly between phyllo shells. Sprinkle with parsley; serve immediately. *Makes 5 servings (3 shells each)*

# Hot & Sweet Deviled Eggs

6 hard-cooked eggs, peeled and halved lengthwise
4 to 5 tablespoons mayonnaise
$\frac{1}{4}$ teaspoon curry powder
$\frac{1}{4}$ teaspoon black pepper
$\frac{1}{8}$ teaspoon salt
  Dash of paprika
$\frac{1}{4}$ cup sweetened dried cherries, finely chopped
1 teaspoon minced fresh chives
  Fresh chives (optional)

1. Scoop egg yolks into bowl; reserve whites. Mash yolks and mayonnaise until creamy. Stir in curry powder, pepper, salt and paprika; mix well. Add cherries and minced chives.

2. Pipe or spoon yolk mixture into egg whites. Garnish with chives.

*Makes 12 servings*

# Spicy Margarita Shrimp

$^2/_3$ cup *Frank's® RedHot® Chile 'n Lime™* Hot Sauce
$^1/_4$ cup olive oil
2 tablespoons lime juice
1 teaspoon grated lime zest
2 teaspoons minced garlic
$1^1/_2$ pounds jumbo shrimp, shelled and deveined
1 (16-ounce) jar mild chunky salsa
2 tablespoons minced cilantro
2 red or orange bell peppers, cut into chunks

1. Whisk together *Chile 'n Lime™* Hot Sauce, oil, lime juice, zest and garlic. Place shrimp into resealable plastic bag. Pour $^2/_3$ cup marinade over shrimp. Seal bag; marinate in refrigerator 30 minutes.

2. Combine remaining marinade with salsa and cilantro in bowl; set aside.

3. Place shrimp and bell pepper chunks on metal skewers. Grill over medium-high direct heat about 8 minutes until shrimp turn pink. Serve with spicy salsa on the side. *Makes 4 to 6 servings*

Prep Time: **10 minutes**
Cook Time: **8 minutes**
Marinate Time: **30 minutes**

# Beer-Battered Mushrooms

1 cup all-purpose flour
$\frac{1}{2}$ teaspoon baking powder
$\frac{1}{2}$ teaspoon chili powder
$\frac{1}{4}$ teaspoon salt
$\frac{1}{8}$ teaspoon black pepper
1 cup beer
1 egg, separated
1 pound small mushrooms
$1\frac{1}{2}$ quarts vegetable oil
Additional salt

1. Mix flour, baking powder, chili powder, $\frac{1}{4}$ teaspoon salt and black pepper in medium bowl. Whisk together beer and egg yolk in small bowl. Wipe mushrooms clean with damp cloth or paper towel.

2. Beat egg whites in large bowl with electric mixer at medium speed until soft peaks form. Heat oil in 4-quart saucepan to 365°F.

3. Stir beer mixture into flour mixture just until blended. Fold in egg whites.

4. Dip mushrooms, 4 to 5 at a time, into batter and place carefully in hot oil. Fry mushrooms in batches, turning with tongs or slotted spoon until all sides are golden brown. Remove mushrooms to paper towels to drain. Sprinkle immediately with additional salt. (Do not allow oil temperature to dip below 365°F or rise above 375°F.) Stir batter between batches. Serve hot. *Makes 6 to 8 servings*

# Chipotle Chicken Quesadillas

1 package (8 ounces) cream cheese, softened
1 cup (4 ounces) shredded Mexican cheese blend
1 tablespoon minced chipotle peppers in adobo sauce
5 (10-inch) burrito-size flour tortillas
1¼ pounds cooked chicken, shredded
    Nonstick cooking spray
    Fresh chopped cilantro (optional)
    Guacamole (optional)
    Sour cream (optional)
    Salsa (optional)

1. Combine cheeses and chipotle peppers in large bowl.

2. Spread ⅓ cup cream cheese mixture over half of tortilla. Top with about 1 cup chicken. Fold over tortilla. Repeat with remaining tortillas.

3. Heat large nonstick skillet over medium-high heat. Spray outside surface of each tortilla with cooking spray. Cook each tortilla 4 to 6 minutes or until lightly browned, turning once during cooking.

4. Cut each tortilla into 4 wedges. Garnish with cilantro. Serve with guacamole, sour cream and salsa, if desired.

*Makes 5 servings (4 wedges each)*

Any leftover chipotle peppers in adobo sauce should be transferred to a nonmetal or nonreactive container and stored in the refrigerator. This helps prevent flavor changes.

# Poblano Pepper Kabobs

1 large poblano pepper*
4 ounces smoked turkey breast, cut into 8 cubes
4 ounces pepper jack cheese, chilled and cut into 8 cubes
¼ cup salsa (optional)

*Poblano peppers can sting and irritate the skin, so wear rubber gloves when handling peppers and do not touch your eyes.

1. Preheat toaster oven to 400°F. Soak 4 wooden skewers in cold water 10 minutes. Drain and set aside. Place pepper in pan of boiling water. Cook for 1 minute. Drain well. Core, seed and cut pepper into 12 bite-size pieces.

2. Thread 1 piece pepper, 1 piece turkey and 1 piece cheese. Repeat, ending with pepper. Repeat with remaining 3 skewers.

3. Place kabobs on toaster oven baking pan. Bake 3 minutes or until cheese starts to melt. Remove immediately. Serve with salsa, if desired.

*Makes 4 servings*

# Micro Mini Stuffed Potatoes

**1 pound small new potatoes, scrubbed**
**1/4 cup sour cream**
**2 tablespoons butter, softened**
**1/2 teaspoon minced garlic**
**1/4 cup milk**
**1/2 cup (2 ounces) shredded sharp Cheddar cheese**
**1/2 teaspoon salt**
**1/4 teaspoon black pepper**
**1/4 cup finely chopped green onions (optional)**

1. Pierce potatoes with fork in several places. Microwave potatoes on HIGH 5 to 6 minutes or until tender. Let stand 5 minutes; cut in half lengthwise. Scoop out pulp from potatoes and place in medium bowl.

2. Beat potato pulp with electric mixer at low speed 30 seconds. Add sour cream, butter and garlic; beat until well blended. Gradually add milk, beating until smooth. Add cheese, salt and pepper; beat until blended.

3. Fill each potato shell with equal amounts of potato mixture. Microwave on HIGH 1 to 2 minutes or just until cheese melts. Garnish with green onions.

*Makes 4 servings*

# Soy-Braised Chicken Wings

2 tablespoons dry sherry

2 tablespoons soy sauce

1 tablespoon sugar

1 tablespoon cornstarch

3 cloves minced garlic, divided

1 teaspoon red pepper flakes

12 chicken wings (about 2½ pounds), tips removed and cut into halves

2 tablespoons vegetable oil

3 green onions, cut into 1-inch pieces

¼ cup chicken broth

1 teaspoon sesame oil

1 tablespoon sesame seeds, toasted

1. For marinade, combine sherry, soy sauce, sugar, cornstarch, two cloves garlic and red pepper flakes in large bowl; mix well. Stir in chicken wings; cover and marinate overnight in refrigerator, turning once or twice.

2. Drain wings, reserving marinade. Heat wok over high heat 1 minute. Add vegetable oil and heat 30 seconds. Add half of wings; cook 10 to 15 minutes or until wings are brown on all sides, turning occasionally. Remove with slotted spoon to bowl; set aside. Reheat oil in wok 30 seconds and repeat with remaining wings. Reduce heat to medium. Pour off any remaining oil.

3. Add remaining garlic and green onions to wok; cook and stir 30 seconds. Add wings and chicken broth. Cover and cook 5 minutes or until wings are tender, stirring occasionally.

4. Add reserved marinade and stir-fry wings 1 minute until glazed with marinade. Add sesame oil; mix well. Transfer to serving platter; sprinkle with sesame seeds.                    *Makes 2 dozen wings*

# Stromboli Sticks

  1 package (13.8 ounces) refrigerated pizza crust dough
10 mozzarella cheese sticks
30 thin slices pepperoni
  1 jar (1 pound 10 ounces) RAGÚ® Old World Style® Pasta Sauce, heated

1. Preheat oven to 425°F. Grease baking sheet; set aside.

2. Roll pizza dough into 13×10-inch rectangle. Cut in half crosswise, then cut each half into 5 strips.

3. Arrange 1 cheese stick on each strip of pizza dough, then top with 3 slices pepperoni. Fold edges over, sealing tightly.

4. Arrange stromboli sticks on prepared baking sheet, seam side down. Bake 15 minutes or until golden. Serve with Pasta Sauce for dipping.

*Makes 10 sticks*

Prep Time: **15 minutes**
Cook Time: **15 minutes**

# Crostini with Lemony Pesto

  1 (4-ounce) French baguette
  3 tablespoons prepared pesto
$^1/_2$ teaspoon lemon juice
$^1/_2$ cup chopped plum tomato

1. Preheat oven to 350°F.

2. Cut baguette crosswise into 16 slices; arrange on baking sheet. Bake 11 to 12 minutes or until bread begins to brown. Cool completely.

3. Combine pesto and lemon juice in small bowl; stir until well blended. Spread each bread slice with $^1/_2$ teaspoon pesto mixture. Top with tomato. Serve immediately.

*Makes 8 servings*

Party Starters

43

# Salad

## sensations

# Fruit Salad with Cherry Vinaigrette

**Cherry Vinaigrette**

$1/2$ cup fresh sweet cherries, pitted and chopped

$1/4$ cup orange juice

1 to 2 tablespoons honey

2 tablespoons balsamic vinegar

1 tablespoon canola oil

Pinch of salt

**Fruit Salad**

3 cups cantaloupe, diced

1 large mango, peeled and diced

$1/4$ cup almonds, sliced

1. For vinaigrette, combine cherries, orange juice, honey, balsamic vinegar, oil and salt in small bowl. Stir well; set aside.

2. Combine cantaloupe and mango in large bowl. Add dressing just before serving; stir well. Sprinkle with almonds. *Makes 8 servings*

Variation: Substitute peaches or nectarines for mango. If fresh cherries are not available, use frozen cherries, thawed and well drained.

# Rice and Bean Salad

1 can (about 14 ounces) chicken broth
2 cups uncooked instant brown rice
1 tablespoon olive oil
1 medium onion, chopped
3 cloves garlic, minced
2 medium carrots, cut into matchstick-size strips
1 medium zucchini, halved lengthwise and sliced
1 can (about 14 ounces) Italian-style stewed tomatoes
1 can (about 15 ounces) red beans, drained
$\frac{1}{2}$ cup (2 ounces) grated Parmesan cheese
$\frac{1}{2}$ cup Italian salad dressing
$\frac{1}{4}$ cup finely chopped fresh basil leaves
   Black pepper

1. Bring chicken broth to a boil in medium saucepan over high heat; add rice and cover. Reduce heat and cook 10 minutes or until chicken broth is absorbed. Remove from heat; set aside.

2. Heat oil in large skillet over medium-high heat. Add onion and garlic; cook and stir 2 to 3 minutes or until onion is tender. Add carrots and zucchini; cook and stir 3 to 4 minutes or until vegetables are crisp-tender. Remove from heat. Add tomatoes, beans and rice; stir to combine.

3. Place rice mixture in large bowl. Cover with plastic wrap and refrigerate overnight.

4. To serve, add Parmesan cheese, salad dressing and basil to rice mixture; toss lightly. Season with black pepper.                      *Makes 6 servings*

Serving Suggestion: Serve with breadsticks or croissants and slices of watermelon.

Make-Ahead Time: up to 2 days before serving
Final Prep Time: 5 minutes

# Bean & Mushroom Salad with Fresh Herb Dressing

1 can (about 15 ounces) red kidney beans, rinsed and drained
1 can (about 15 ounces) lima beans, rinsed and drained
1 cup sliced mushrooms
1 cup chopped green bell pepper
$\frac{1}{4}$ cup chopped green onions
Fresh Herb Dressing (recipe follows)
1 cup cherry tomatoes, halved
10 leaves romaine lettuce (optional)

1. Combine kidney beans, lima beans, mushrooms, bell pepper and green onions in large bowl. Prepare Fresh Herb Dressing. Add dressing to vegetable mixture; toss to coat. Cover; refrigerate 2 to 3 hours or overnight.

2. Add tomatoes to bean mixture; mix well. Serve on lettuce-lined plates, if desired.                    *Makes 10 servings*

## Fresh Herb Dressing

$\frac{1}{2}$ cup red wine vinegar
2 tablespoons olive oil
1 clove garlic, crushed
1 tablespoon chopped fresh oregano
1 tablespoon chopped fresh marjoram
$\frac{1}{2}$ teaspoon sugar
$\frac{1}{8}$ teaspoon black pepper

Combine all ingredients in small bowl; mix well.

# Mixed Greens with Cranberry Balsamic Vinaigrette

 ½ cup pecan halves
 1 bag (4 ounces) mixed spring greens
 ½ cup dried sweetened cranberries
 ½ cup thinly sliced red onion
 ¼ cup vegetable oil
 2 tablespoons soy sauce
 2 to 3 tablespoons balsamic vinegar
 2 tablespoons packed dark brown sugar
 1 teaspoon grated fresh ginger
 ½ teaspoon red pepper flakes
 ½ cup (2 ounces) crumbled blue cheese or goat cheese

1. Heat medium skillet over medium-high heat. Add pecans and cook 2 to 3 minutes or until just beginning to lightly brown, stirring constantly. Set aside to cool.

2. Combine greens, cranberries and onion in large bowl. Combine oil, soy sauce, vinegar, sugar, ginger and red pepper flakes in small bowl. Whisk until well blended.

3. Pour dressing over lettuce mixture; toss gently. Top with pecans and cheese. *Makes 4 servings*

# Traditional German Potato Salad

$2\frac{1}{2}$ pounds red potatoes
$\frac{1}{4}$ pound bacon, cut into small pieces
$\frac{1}{2}$ medium onion, finely chopped
$\frac{1}{2}$ cup cider vinegar
$\frac{1}{4}$ cup water
1 tablespoon plus 1 teaspoon sugar
1 teaspoon salt
1 teaspoon brown mustard seeds
1 teaspoon mustard
2 tablespoons finely chopped fresh parsley
1 teaspoon paprika

1. Place potatoes in large saucepan. Add enough water to cover. Bring to a boil over high heat. Reduce heat and simmer, uncovered, 20 to 30 minutes or until potatoes are fork-tender. Drain. Let potatoes cool.

2. Meanwhile, cook bacon in medium skillet over medium heat until crisp. Remove with slotted spoon. Crumble into small bowl; set aside.

3. Cook and stir onion in 3 tablespoons bacon drippings until tender. Peel potatoes and cut into $\frac{1}{4}$-inch slices.

4. Combine vinegar, water, sugar, salt, mustard seeds and mustard in large bowl. Add potatoes and bacon to vinegar mixture; toss to coat evenly. Top with parsley and sprinkle with paprika. Serve hot or cold.

*Makes 6 to 8 servings*

Note: This salad contains no eggs or mayonnaise and will keep well for picnics and other outdoor meals.

# ABC Slaw

2 green apples, cut into thin strips
1 package (10 ounces) broccoli slaw with carrots
3 stalks celery, cut into thin slices
1 bulb fennel, cut into thin strips
$\frac{1}{4}$ cup creamy salad dressing
1 tablespoon lemon juice
$\frac{1}{2}$ teaspoon red pepper flakes

Combine all ingredients in large bowl; mix well. Chill 1 hour before serving.

*Makes 4 to 6 servings*

# Peppy Palermo Pasta Salad

$\frac{1}{2}$ pound rotini pasta
2 zucchini, cut in half lengthwise, sliced
1 red bell pepper, cut into thin strips
$\frac{1}{4}$ cup chopped red onion
2 cloves garlic, minced
$\frac{3}{4}$ teaspoon Italian seasoning
$\frac{1}{3}$ cup plus 2 tablespoons olive oil, divided
　Juice and grated peel of 1 lemon
2 tablespoons minced fresh parsley
$\frac{3}{4}$ teaspoon hot pepper sauce
$\frac{1}{4}$ teaspoon salt (optional)
$\frac{3}{4}$ cup (3 ounces) SARGENTO® Fancy Parmesan Shredded Cheese

Cook pasta according to package directions; drain. In large skillet, sauté zucchini, bell pepper, onion, garlic and Italian seasoning in 2 tablespoons oil just until crisp-tender; cool. In large bowl, combine vegetable mixture and pasta; chill several hours. Just before serving, whisk together remaining $\frac{1}{3}$ cup oil, lemon juice, lemon peel, parsley, pepper sauce and salt. Pour over pasta mixture. Add cheese; toss to coat thoroughly.

*Makes 6 servings*

# Rotini Salad

10 ounces uncooked rotini
2 to 3 stalks broccoli
1 can (6 ounces) small pitted black olives, drained
10 to 12 cherry tomatoes, cut into halves
$\frac{1}{2}$ medium red onion, thinly sliced
$\frac{1}{2}$ cup Italian salad dressing
1 to 2 tablespoons grated Parmesan cheese
Salt and black pepper
Carrot strips (optional)

1. Cook pasta according to package directions. Drain in colander. Cover and refrigerate until chilled.

2. Trim and peel broccoli stalks into 1-inch pieces. Cut broccoli into florets.

3. To cook broccoli, bring 1 quart lightly salted water to a boil in 2-quart saucepan over high heat. Immediately add broccoli; return to a boil. Continue boiling, uncovered, 3 to 5 minutes until bright green and tender. Drain broccoli; rinse under cold water and drain thoroughly.

4. Combine pasta, broccoli, olives, tomatoes, onion and salad dressing in large bowl. Stir in cheese. Season to taste with salt and pepper. Toss gently to coat.

5. Cover; refrigerate at least 2 hours. Garnish with carrot strips.

*Makes 8 to 10 servings*

# Kohlrabi and Carrot Slaw

2 pounds kohlrabi bulbs, peeled and shredded

2 medium carrots, shredded

1 small red bell pepper, chopped

8 cherry tomatoes, cut into halves

2 green onions, thinly sliced

$1/4$ cup mayonnaise

$1/4$ cup plain yogurt

2 tablespoons cider vinegar

2 tablespoons finely chopped fresh parsley

1 teaspoon dried dill weed

$1/4$ teaspoon ground cumin

$1/4$ teaspoon salt

$1/8$ teaspoon black pepper

1. Combine kohlrabi, carrots, bell pepper, tomatoes and green onions in medium bowl.

2. Combine mayonnaise, yogurt, vinegar, parsley, dill, cumin, salt and black pepper in small bowl until smooth. Add to vegetables; toss to coat. Refrigerate, covered, until ready to serve. *Makes 8 servings*

# Waldorf Sweet Potato Salad

**Salad**
- 1/3 cup walnuts
- 3 cups grated peeled sweet potato
- 1 red apple, unpeeled, cored and coarsely chopped
- 1/2 cup chopped celery
- 1/2 cup red seedless grapes, cut in half
- 1/3 cup crumbled blue cheese (optional)
  - Red leaf lettuce leaves (optional)

**Dressing**
- 3 tablespoons apple juice
- 2 tablespoons vegetable oil
- 1 tablespoon plus 1 teaspoon white wine vinegar
- 1 teaspoon sugar
- 1/2 teaspoon salt

Toast walnuts in oven or toaster oven at 350°F until golden, about 10 minutes. Cool. Place walnuts, sweet potatoes, apple, celery, grapes, and blue cheese, if desired, in large bowl.

To make dressing, whisk apple juice, oil, vinegar, sugar and salt until blended. Pour over salad and toss well. If desired, serve on red leaf lettuce leaves. *Makes 6 servings*

Favorite recipe from **North Carolina SweetPotato Commission**

# Mediterranean Veggie Salad

2 ounces uncooked whole wheat rotini
$1/2$ cup (3 ounces) seeded and diced tomatoes
$1/2$ cup (2 ounces) thinly sliced zucchini
$1/2$ cup thinly sliced green bell pepper
$1/4$ cup finely chopped red onion
2 tablespoons coarsely chopped pimiento-stuffed green olives
1 teaspoon dried oregano
$1/2$ teaspoon dried basil
$1/2$ clove garlic, minced
2 to 3 teaspoons cider vinegar
1 teaspoon extra-virgin olive oil
$1/4$ teaspoon salt
2 ounces feta cheese, crumbled

1. Cook pasta according to package directions; drain. Rinse under cold water until completely cooled; drain.

2. Meanwhile, combine tomatoes, zucchini, bell pepper, onion, olives, oregano, basil, garlic and vinegar in large bowl; toss well.

3. Add cooled pasta, oil and salt to tomato mixture; toss gently. Top with cheese; do not stir. *Makes 5 servings*

Prep Time: **11 minutes**

# Tex-Mex Potato Salad

2 pounds red potatoes, cut into $\frac{1}{2}$-inch dice
Salt
1 cup *French's® Gourmayo™* Smoked Chipotle Light Mayonnaise
2 tablespoons red wine vinegar
1$\frac{1}{2}$ cups finely cut-up vegetables such as celery, red bell pepper, red onion and green chilies
$\frac{1}{2}$ cup frozen whole kernel corn, thawed
1 can (2$\frac{1}{4}$ ounces) sliced black olives ($\frac{1}{2}$ cup)

1. Place potatoes in large saucepan. Cover with water. Add salt to taste. Boil for 10 to 12 minutes or until tender. Drain well and cool.

2. Combine mayonnaise and vinegar in large bowl. Add potatoes and remaining ingredients. Toss until vegetables are well-coated. Cover and chill to blend flavors.                *Makes about 6 cups*

Prep Time: **10 minutes**
Cook Time: **10 minutes**

Store potatoes in a cool, dark, dry, well-ventilated place. Do not refrigerate potatoes. It is important to protect potatoes from light because it can cause them to turn green and lose quality.

# Rustic Dried Cherry Salad

3 cups cubed French bread

$1/4$ cup pecans or toasted walnuts, chopped

$1/2$ cup dried sweetened cherries, chopped

1 celery stalk, trimmed and diced

3 tablespoons canola oil *or* $1^1/2$ tablespoons canola oil and $1^1/2$ tablespoons olive oil

3 tablespoons raspberry vinegar

1 tablespoon honey

2 tablespoons water

$1/4$ teaspoon curry powder

1. Preheat oven to 350°F. Spread bread cubes on baking sheet; bake 15 minutes or until toasted. Cool completely. Set aside.

2. Toast pecans in medium skillet over medium heat 3 minutes, stirring frequently.

3. Combine pecans, cherries, celery and bread in large bowl.

4. Combine oil, vinegar, honey, water and curry powder in cup. Stir well. Pour over salad and toss. Serve immediately. *Makes 4 servings*

# Southwestern Salad

1 can (about 15 ounces) black beans, rinsed and drained
1½ cups cooked corn kernels
1½ cups chopped seeded tomato
½ cup thinly sliced green onions
¼ cup minced fresh cilantro
½ cup oil
2 tablespoons red wine vinegar
1 teaspoon salt
½ teaspoon black pepper

1. Combine beans, corn, tomato, green onions and cilantro in large bowl.

2. Whisk together oil, vinegar, salt and black pepper. Pour dressing over salad; stir gently to combine. Serve at room temperature or slightly chilled.

*Makes 6 servings*

# Tomato Potato Salad

1½ pounds fresh California tomatoes, seeded and cubed
½ cup chopped red onion
¼ cup chopped fresh cilantro
1½ teaspoons ground cumin
1 teaspoon chopped fresh garlic
¼ teaspoon black pepper
1½ pounds red potatoes, cooked and cubed
½ cup plain yogurt

Combine tomatoes, onion and seasonings in large bowl. Add potatoes and yogurt; gently toss to coat. *Makes 6 to 8 servings*

Favorite recipe from **California Tomato Commission**

# Marinated Bean and Vegetable Salad

$1/4$ cup orange juice

3 tablespoons white wine vinegar

1 tablespoon canola or vegetable oil

2 cloves garlic, minced

1 can (about 15 ounces) Great Northern beans, rinsed and drained

1 can (about 15 ounces) kidney beans, rinsed and drained

$1/4$ cup coarsely chopped red cabbage

$1/4$ cup chopped red onion

$1/4$ cup chopped green bell pepper

$1/4$ cup chopped red bell pepper

$1/4$ cup sliced celery

1. For dressing, combine orange juice, vinegar, oil and garlic in small bowl with tight-fitting lid; shake well.

2. Combine beans, cabbage, onion, bell peppers and celery in large bowl. Pour dressing over bean mixture; toss to coat.

3. Refrigerate, covered, 1 to 2 hours to allow flavors to blend. Toss before serving. *Makes 8 servings*

# Newman's Fantastic Five
## Food Group Salad

1 pound small shells or elbow macaroni, cooked (8 cups), divided
1 cup (4 ounces) finely grated Romano or Parmesan cheese, divided
1 (15½- to 19-ounce) can chickpeas, rinsed and drained
5 medium ribs celery, cut into ¼-inch pieces (2 cups)
2 cups shredded carrots
1 (11-ounce) jar NEWMAN'S OWN® Mild Salsa
2 medium apples, peeled, cored and cut into ¼-inch pieces (2 cups)
2 medium pears, peeled, cored and cut into ¼-inch pieces (2 cups)
1½ pounds small tomatoes (about 7)
1 large red onion, minced (1 cup)
1 (15½- to 19-ounce) can white kidney beans (cannellini), rinsed and drained
1 large cucumber, peeled and cut into ¼-inch pieces
1 cup (4 ounces) shredded Cheddar cheese
1 cup (8 ounces) NEWMAN'S OWN® Olive Oil & Vinegar Salad Dressing

In large bowl, layer ingredients in the following order (use entire quantity unless otherwise noted): 4 cups pasta, ½ cup Romano cheese, chickpeas, celery, carrots, salsa, 4 cups pasta, ½ cup Romano cheese, apples, pears, tomatoes, onion, cannellini beans, cucumber and Cheddar cheese.

Cover with salad dressing. Let stand 15 minutes before serving or cover and refrigerate to serve later. *Makes 12 servings*

# Pea Salad with Pasta and Cheese

2 cups macaroni, uncooked
1 box (10 ounces) BIRDS EYE® frozen Green Peas
6 ounces Monterey Jack, Swiss or Cheddar cheese (or any
    combination), cubed
$\frac{1}{2}$ cup mayonnaise
$\frac{1}{4}$ cup sliced green onions
$\frac{1}{2}$ teaspoon celery salt (optional)

• In large saucepan, cook pasta according to package directions. Add peas during last 7 minutes; drain and refrigerate until chilled.

• In large bowl, toss together pasta, peas, cheese, mayonnaise, onions and celery salt, if desired, until blended.    *Makes 4 servings*

Prep Time: **5 minutes**
Cook Time: **12 to 15 minutes**

# Bean Salad with Bulgur

$^3/_4$ cup uncooked dried red kidney beans, sorted and rinsed
$^3/_4$ cup uncooked dried pinto beans, sorted and rinsed
7 cups water, divided
1$^1/_2$ cups (8 ounces) fresh green beans, cut into 2-inch pieces
$^1/_2$ cup uncooked bulgur wheat
$^1/_3$ cup vegetable oil
1 tablespoon dark sesame oil
6 green onions, chopped
2 tablespoons minced fresh ginger
3 cloves garlic, minced
$^1/_4$ teaspoon red pepper flakes
3 tablespoons soy sauce
2 tablespoons white wine vinegar
$^1/_2$ teaspoon sugar

1. Soak kidney and pinto beans overnight in cold water; rinse and drain.
Place in large saucepan and cover with 6 cups water. Bring to a boil.
Reduce heat to low; simmer, covered, 1 hour or until tender. Place green
beans in medium saucepan; cover with water. Bring to a boil over medium-
high heat. Reduce heat to low; simmer, covered, 5 to 6 minutes or until
beans are crisp-tender. Rinse and drain all beans; set aside.

2. Combine bulgur and 1 cup water in small saucepan. Bring to a boil over
medium heat. Reduce heat to low; simmer, covered, 5 to 10 minutes or until
water is absorbed and bulgur is fluffy.

3. Combine green beans, bulgur, kidney and pinto beans in large bowl.

4. Heat oils in large skillet over medium heat. Add green onions, ginger,
garlic and red pepper flakes. Cook and stir about 3 minutes. Remove
from heat. Stir in soy sauce, vinegar and sugar. Pour oil mixture over bean
mixture; mix well. Cover; refrigerate 2 to 3 hours.

*Makes 6 to 8 servings*

# Roasted Vegetable Salad

1 cup sliced mushrooms

1 cup thinly sliced carrots

1 cup chopped green or yellow bell pepper

1 cup cherry tomatoes, halved

$^1/_2$ cup chopped white, Vidalia or other sweet onion

2 tablespoons chopped pitted kalamata olives

2 teaspoons lemon juice, divided

1 teaspoon olive oil

1 teaspoon dried oregano

$^1/_2$ teaspoon black pepper

3 cups packed torn stemmed spinach or baby spinach

**1.** Preheat oven to 375°F. Combine mushrooms, carrots, bell pepper, tomatoes, onion, olives, 1 teaspoon lemon juice, oil, oregano and black pepper in large bowl; toss until evenly coated. Spread vegetables in single layer on baking sheet.

**2.** Bake 20 minutes, stirring once. Remove from oven; stir in remaining 1 teaspoon lemon juice. Serve warm over spinach.          *Makes 2 servings*

# Spicy Peanut Noodle Salad

$1/3$ cup *French's®* Honey Dijon Mustard
$1/3$ cup chicken broth
$1/3$ cup peanut butter
2 tablespoons teriyaki sauce
2 tablespoons *Frank's® RedHot®* Cayenne Pepper Sauce, or more to taste
2 cups thinly sliced vegetables, such as green onion, snow peas, cucumber or bell peppers
4 ounces thin spaghetti, cooked and drained ($1^1/2$ cups cooked)

1. Combine mustard, chicken broth, peanut butter, teriyaki sauce and **Frank's RedHot** Sauce in large bowl; whisk until blended.

2. Add vegetables and pasta; toss to coat. Serve immediately. If desired, serve on salad greens. *Makes 4 servings*

Prep Time: **10 minutes**

Try serving this salad as a main dish. Simply add 2 cups diced cooked chicken or turkey with the vegetables and pasta before tossing.

# Grilled Beet Salad

6 medium red beets (about 1$\frac{1}{2}$ pounds), peeled
1 medium yellow onion, cut into $\frac{1}{2}$-inch wedges
$\frac{1}{2}$ pound carrots, halved lengthwise and cut into 1-inch pieces
$\frac{1}{4}$ cup plus 2 tablespoons olive oil, divided
3 to 4 tablespoons balsamic vinegar
$\frac{1}{2}$ teaspoon dried rosemary, crushed
1 clove garlic, minced
$\frac{1}{2}$ teaspoon salt
$\frac{1}{4}$ teaspoon black pepper
6 cups chopped spring greens
2 ounces Gorgonzola or goat cheese, crumbled
1 cup pecan pieces, toasted*

*Spread pecans in a single layer on a baking sheet and toast in a preheated 350°F oven for 8 to 10 minutes or until very lightly browned.*

1. Prepare grill for direct cooking over medium-high heat.

2. Cut beets into 1-inch pieces and place in microwavable dish. Cover with plastic wrap and microwave on HIGH 6 to 8 minutes until slightly soft. Remove from microwave, uncover and cool. Pat beets dry with paper towels when cool.

3. Divide beets, onions and carrots evenly between two 12×8 disposable foil pans. Drizzle each pan with 1 tablespoon oil, stirring to coat all vegetables. Arrange vegetables in single layer. Cover loosely with foil. Grill 22 to 25 minutes, stirring every few minutes until fork-tender. Remove from grill. Place on cooling rack. Cool completely.

4. For vinaigrette, combine remaining $\frac{1}{4}$ cup oil, vinegar, rosemary, garlic, salt and pepper in small bowl; mix well.

5. Place greens in large bowl. Top with vegetables; drizzle with vinaigrette. Sprinkle with cheese and pecans. *Makes 4 servings*

# Wheat Berry Apple Salad

    1 cup uncooked wheat berries (whole wheat kernels)
    $1/2$ teaspoon salt
    2 apples (1 red and 1 green)
    $1/2$ cup dried cranberries
    $1/3$ cup chopped walnuts
    1 stalk celery, chopped
    Grated peel and juice of 1 medium orange
    2 tablespoons rice wine vinegar
    $1^{1}/_{2}$ tablespoons chopped fresh mint
    Lettuce leaves (optional)

1. Place wheat berries and salt in large saucepan; cover with 1-inch water.* Bring to a boil. Stir and reduce heat to low. Cover and cook, stirring occasionally, 45 minutes to 1 hour or until wheat berries are tender, but chewy. (Add additional water if wheat berries become dry during cooking.) Drain and let cool. (Refrigerate for up to 4 days if not using immediately.)

2. Cut unpeeled apples into bite-size pieces. Combine wheat berries, apples, cranberries, walnuts, celery, orange peel, orange juice, vinegar and mint in large bowl. Stir to combine. Cover; refrigerate at least 1 hour to allow flavors to blend. Serve on lettuce leaves.          *Makes about 6 cups*

*To cut cooking time by 20 to 30 minutes, wheat berries may be soaked in water overnight. Drain and cover with 1 inch of fresh water before cooking.*

# Spinach, Cheese & Walnut Salad

1 package (8 ounces) cream cheese
1 cup walnuts, chopped
$\frac{1}{2}$ pound packed torn stemmed spinach
3 stalks celery, sliced
1 piece cucumber (about 2 inches), diced
1 Granny Smith or red apple, cored and diced
$\frac{1}{4}$ cup lemon juice
$\frac{1}{4}$ cup walnut or safflower oil
   Salt and black pepper

1. Roll cheese into balls, using about 1 teaspoonful for each. Lightly roll balls in chopped walnuts. Refrigerate cheese balls until ready to serve.

2. Combine spinach, celery and cucumber in serving bowl. Toss apple and lemon juice in small bowl; add apple to spinach mixture, reserving lemon juice.

3. Blend oil, salt and pepper into reserved lemon juice; pour over spinach mixture. Toss to coat. Just before serving, place cheese balls in salad.

*Makes 4 servings*

# Potato Beet Salad

1 pound potatoes, peeled and cut into $\frac{1}{2}$-inch chunks
1 can (14.5 ounces) beets, drained and cut into $\frac{1}{2}$-inch pieces
1 cup HELLMANN'S® or BEST FOODS® Real Mayonnaise
1 package (10 ounces) frozen mixed vegetables, thawed and drained
3 large green onions, finely chopped
   Juice of 1 lime

1. In 2-quart saucepan, combine potatoes with enough salted water to cover. Bring to a boil over high heat. Reduce heat and simmer 12 minutes or until potatoes are tender. Drain and cool.

2. In large bowl, combine potatoes and beets with remaining ingredients. Season to taste with salt and ground black pepper. Chill, if desired. Serve on a bed of lettuce garnished with sliced hard cooked eggs and sliced black olives, if desired. *Makes 8 servings*

Variation: Use 1 pound fresh beets and in 2-quart saucepan, combine beets with enough water to cover. Bring to a boil over high heat. Reduce heat and simmer 15 minutes or until beets are tender. Drain and cool; then peel and cut into $\frac{1}{2}$-inch pieces.

Prep Time: **15 minutes**
Cook Time: **15 minutes**

Salad Sensations

# Main
*attractions*

# Glazed Ham and Sweet Potato Kabobs

**1 large sweet potato (12 ounces), peeled**
**$\frac{1}{4}$ cup water**
**1 ham slice (12 ounces), $\frac{1}{4}$ inch thick**
**16 fresh pineapple chunks (about 1 inch)**
**$\frac{1}{4}$ cup ($\frac{1}{2}$ stick) butter or margarine**
**$\frac{1}{4}$ cup packed dark brown sugar**
**2 tablespoons cider vinegar**
**2 tablespoons molasses**
**1 tablespoon yellow mustard**
**1 tablespoon Worcestershire sauce**
**$\frac{3}{4}$ teaspoon ground cinnamon**
**$\frac{1}{2}$ teaspoon ground allspice**
**$\frac{1}{8}$ teaspoon red pepper flakes**
**1 package (10 ounces) prepared mixed salad greens**

1. Lightly brush grid with oil. Prepare grill for direct cooking over high heat.

2. Cut sweet potato into 16 pieces and place in shallow microwavable dish with water. Cover with plastic wrap and microwave on HIGH 4 minutes or until fork-tender. Drain. Spread potatoes in single layer and cool about 5 minutes.

3. Cut ham slice into 20 (1-inch) pieces. Set aside with cooled sweet potatoes and pineapple chunks.

4. For the glaze, combine butter, brown sugar, vinegar, molasses, mustard, Worcestershire sauce, cinnamon, allspice and red pepper flakes in medium saucepan. Bring to a boil over high heat. Reduce heat to medium-high. Continue to boil 2 minutes or until sauce reduces to $\frac{1}{2}$ cup. Remove from heat and cool.

5. Thread ham, potato and pineapple, starting and ending each skewer with ham, onto 4 (12-inch) wooden skewers.*

6. Arrange skewers on grid. Cover and cook 2 minutes; baste evenly with half of sauce. Turn and cook 2 minutes more; brush with remaining sauce. Cook, turning every 2 minutes, until potatoes are brown. Remove from heat and let stand 5 minutes before serving.

7. To serve, place mixed greens on platter. Remove ham, sweet potato and pineapple from skewers and place on top of greens. Serve immediately.

*Makes 4 servings*

*Soak wooden skewers in water 20 minutes before using to prevent burning.*

Serving Suggestion: Toast 6 to 8 large marshmallows on skewers alongside the kabobs. Separate the sweet potatoes and top with warm marshmallows.

## Crunchy Pecan Chicken

  4 boneless, skinless chicken breast halves
  4 teaspoons honey mustard
$1/3$ cup finely chopped pecans
$1/3$ cup Italian seasoned bread crumbs
  2 tablespoons butter or margarine, melted
$1/4$ teaspoon salt

Arrange chicken in a single layer in a shallow baking pan. Brush top of each chicken piece with one teaspoon honey mustard. In a small bowl, mix together pecans, bread crumbs, butter and salt. Sprinkle nut mixture evenly over chicken. Bake in 400°F. oven 30 minutes or until chicken is browned and fork-tender.

*Makes 4 servings*

Favorite recipe from **Delmarva Poultry Industry, Inc.**

# Cocoa-Coffee Spiced Chicken with Salsa Mole

2 tablespoons ground coffee
2 tablespoons HERSHEY'S Cocoa
1 tablespoon *each* salt and brown sugar
1 teaspoon chili powder
4 boneless, skinless chicken breasts
1 tablespoon vegetable oil
  Salsa Mole (recipe follows)
  Cilantro sprigs (optional)
  Black beans and rice (optional)

1. Heat oven to 425°F. Grease baking sheet.

2. Stir together coffee, cocoa, salt, brown sugar and chili powder. Rub chicken pieces with vegetable oil; pat on cocoa mixture. Place coated chicken pieces on prepared baking sheet.

3. Bake 20 to 25 minutes or until juices are clear. Meanwhile, prepare Salsa Mole.

4. Arrange chicken and salsa on large platter. Garnish with cilantro sprigs, if desired. Serve with black beans and rice, if desired.     *Makes 4 servings*

## Salsa Mole

2 tomatoes, chopped
1 avocado, peeled and diced
1 green onion, minced
1 tablespoon snipped cilantro
1 clove garlic, pressed
¼ cup HERSHEY'S MINI CHIPS™ Semi-Sweet Chocolate Chips
1 teaspoon lime juice

Stir together tomatoes, avocado, onion, cilantro, garlic, chocolate chips and lime juice in medium bowl.     *Makes about 3 cups*

# Spicy Peanut-Coconut Shrimp

$^1/_4$ **cup shredded coconut**

 2 **teaspoons dark sesame oil**

 1 **pound large raw shrimp, peeled, deveined and patted dry**

$^1/_4$ **to** $^1/_2$ **teaspoon red pepper flakes**

 2 **tablespoons chopped fresh mint or cilantro**

$^1/_4$ **cup chopped lightly salted roasted peanuts**

    **Lime wedges (optional)**

1. Toast coconut in small nonstick skillet over medium-high heat 2 to 3 minutes until golden, stirring constantly. Immediately remove from skillet.

2. Heat oil in large nonstick skillet over medium-high heat. Add shrimp and red pepper flakes; stir-fry 3 to 4 minutes until shrimp are pink and opaque. Add mint; toss well and transfer to serving plates. Top each serving with 1 tablespoon toasted coconut and 1 tablespoon chopped peanuts. Garnish with lime wedges. *Makes 4 (3-ounce) servings*

Serving Suggestion: Serve with steamed sugar snap peas, couscous and slices of ripe pineapple.

# Cashew Beef

2 tablespoons cooking oil

8 ounces beef (flank steak, skirt steak, top sirloin or fillet mignon), cut into strips $1/4$ inch thick

3 tablespoons LEE KUM KEE® Premium Brand, Panda Brand or Choy Sun Oyster Sauce

$1/4$ cup red bell pepper strips

$1/4$ cup green bell pepper strips

2 stalks celery, cut into $1/2$-inch slices

$1/2$ cup carrot slices ($1/2$-inch slices)

$1/4$ cup small button mushroom halves

2 tablespoons LEE KUM KEE® Soy Sauce

1 green onion, chopped

2 tablespoons cashews, toasted*

1 tablespoon LEE KUM KEE® Chili Garlic Sauce or Sriracha Chili Sauce

*Cashews can be toasted in wok or skillet prior to cooking.

1. Heat wok or skillet over high heat until hot. Add oil, beef and LEE KUM KEE Oyster Sauce; cook until beef is half done.

2. Add bell peppers, celery, carrots, mushrooms and LEE KUM KEE Soy Sauce; stir-fry until vegetables are crisp-tender. Stir in green onion and cashews. Add LEE KUM KEE Chili Garlic Sauce or Sriracha Chili Sauce for spiciness or use as dipping sauce.          *Makes 2 servings*

# Espresso-Bourbon Steaks
## with Mashed Sweet Potatoes

4 beef tenderloin steaks, cut 1 inch thick (about 4 ounces each)
2 to 4 teaspoons coarsely cracked black pepper
   Mashed Sweet Potatoes (recipe follows)
   Steamed green beans

### Espresso-Bourbon Sauce

$\frac{1}{4}$ cup bourbon
$\frac{1}{4}$ cup maple syrup
$\frac{1}{4}$ cup soy sauce
 1 tablespoon fresh lemon juice
 2 teaspoons instant espresso coffee powder
$\frac{1}{8}$ teaspoon black pepper

1. Combine all sauce ingredients, except pepper, in small saucepan; bring to a boil. Reduce heat and simmer, uncovered 12 to 15 minutes or until sauce is thickened and reduced by about half, stirring occasionally. Stir in pepper. Keep warm.

2. Prepare Mashed Sweet Potatoes. Meanwhile press coarsely cracked pepper on both sides of beef steak. Place steaks on grid over medium, ash-covered coals. Grill, uncovered, 13 to 15 minutes for medium rare doneness, turning once.

3. Evenly divide sauce onto 4 plates. Place steak on top of sauce. Serve with Mashed Sweet Potatoes and green beans. *Makes 4 servings*

Mashed Sweet Potatoes: Place 9 ounces peeled and cubed sweet potatoes and 1 teaspoon salt in large saucepan. Cover with water; bring to a boil. Cook 4 to 5 minutes or until potatoes are tender. Drain. Combine potatoes, 2 tablespoons butter, $\frac{1}{8}$ teaspoon salt and $\frac{1}{8}$ teaspoon black pepper. Beat until mashed and smooth.

Favorite recipe from **National Cattlemen's Beef Association on Behalf of The Beef Checkoff**

# Slow Cooker Seafood Bouillabaisse

½ bulb fennel, chopped
1 medium onion, chopped
2 cloves garlic, minced
2 bottles (24 ounces) beer, divided
1 can (28 ounces) tomato purée
8 ounces clam juice
1 bay leaf
½ teaspoon salt
¼ teaspoon black pepper
2 cups water
½ pound red snapper, pin bones removed and cut into 1-inch pieces
8 mussels, scrubbed and debearded
8 cherry stone clams
8 large shrimp, unpeeled
4 lemon wedges
Italian parsley sprigs (optional)

1. Cook fennel, onion and garlic in large skillet over medium-high heat until onion is soft and translucent. Transfer fennel mixture to 5-quart slow cooker; add 1 bottle of beer, tomato purée, clam juice, bay leaf, salt and pepper. Cover, cook on LOW 6 to 8 hours or on HIGH 3 to 4 hours.

2. During last 30 minutes of cooking, pour remaining 1 bottle of beer into large stock pot. Add water. Place steamer insert in stock pot (do not allow water to touch the insert). Bring to boil. Place fish and shellfish into insert. Cover and steam for 4 to 8 minutes, discarding any mussels or clams that do not open.

3. Remove bay leaf from tomato broth. Ladle broth into wide soup bowls. Place mussels, clams, shrimp and fish on top. Squeeze lemon over fish and shellfish. Garnish with parsley sprigs. *Makes 4 servings*

# Plank Salmon with Grilled Citrus Mango

4 salmon fillets (6 ounces each), skin intact

2 teaspoons sugar, divided

1 teaspoon chili powder

$^1/_2$ teaspoon black pepper

$^1/_4$ teaspoon salt

$^1/_4$ teaspoon ground allspice

1 tablespoon lemon juice

1 tablespoon lime juice

2 tablespoons orange juice

2 teaspoons minced fresh ginger

$^1/_4$ cup chopped fresh mint

$^1/_8$ teaspoon red pepper flakes

2 medium mangos, peeled and cut into 1-inch pieces

1 cedar plank (about 15×7 inches, $^1/_2$ inch thick), soaked*

*Soak in water 5 hours or overnight.*

1. Prepare grill for direct cooking over medium-high heat.

2. Rinse and pat dry salmon fillets. Combine 1 teaspoon sugar, chili powder, black pepper, salt and allspice in small bowl. Rub evenly over flesh side of fillets. Set aside.

3. Combine remaining 1 teaspoon sugar, juices, ginger, mint and red pepper flakes in medium bowl. Set aside.

4. Thread mango pieces onto skewers or spread out in grill basket.

5. If using charcoal grill, wait until coals are covered with gray ash to start grilling salmon. If using gas grill, turn heat down to medium. Keep clean spray bottle filled with water nearby in case plank begins to burn. If it flares up, spray lightly with water.

6. Lightly brush grid with oil and place soaked plank on top. Cover, heat until plank smokes and crackles. Place salmon, skin side down, on plank and arrange mango skewers alongside plank. Cover. Grill 6 to 8 minutes, turning skewers frequently, until mango is slightly charred. Remove mango from the grill. Set aside. Cover grill. Continue grilling the salmon 9 to 12 minutes, without turning or until fish begins to flake when tested with fork.

7. Remove plank from grill and transfer salmon to serving platter. Slide mango pieces off skewers and add to mint mixture, tossing gently to coat. Serve immediately alongside salmon.                    *Makes 4 servings*

Tip: Cedar planks can be purchased at gourmet kitchen stores or hardware stores. Be sure to buy untreated wood at least $^1\!/_2$-inch thick. Use each plank for grilling food only once. Used planks may be broken up into wood chips and used to smoke foods.

## Pineapple Teriyaki Chicken

**$^1\!/_2$ small red onion, halved and thinly sliced**
**1 medium green and/or red bell pepper, cut into 1-inch pieces**
**6 boneless, skinless chicken breasts (about 1$^1\!/_2$ pounds)**
**1 can (20 ounces) pineapple rings, drained**
**1 cup LAWRY'S® Teriyaki Marinade, divided**

Preheat oven to 375°F. Spray 13×9×2-inch glass baking dish with nonstick cooking spray; add onion and bell pepper. Arrange chicken over vegetables. Top with pineapple, then drizzle with Marinade. Bake 40 minutes, or until chicken is thoroughly cooked. Spoon pan juices over chicken and vegetables once during baking and again just before serving.

*Makes 6 servings*

Prep Time: 10 minutes
Cook Time: 45 minutes

Main Attractions

# Thai-Style Pork Chops with Cucumber Sauce

3 tablespoons Thai peanut sauce, divided
$\frac{1}{4}$ teaspoon red pepper flakes
4 bone-in pork chops (5 ounces each)
1 container (6 ounces) plain yogurt
$\frac{1}{4}$ cup diced unpeeled cucumber
2 tablespoons chopped red onion
2 tablespoons finely chopped fresh mint or cilantro
1 teaspoon sugar
Mint sprigs (optional)
Cucumber slices (optional)

1. Preheat broiler or prepare grill. Combine 2 tablespoons peanut sauce and red pepper flakes; brush mixture evenly over both sides of pork chops. Let stand while preparing cucumber sauce, or refrigerate up to 4 hours.

2. Combine yogurt, cucumber, red onion, mint and sugar in medium bowl; mix well. Broil chops 4 inches from heat source or grill, covered, over medium coals 4 minutes; turn and cook 3 minutes more or until barely pink in center. Just before removing from heat, baste with remaining 1 tablespoon peanut sauce. Serve chops with cucumber sauce. Garnish with mint sprigs and cucumber slices.                    *Makes 4 servings*

# Garlicky Oven-Fried Chicken Thighs

1 egg
2 tablespoons water
1 cup plain bread crumbs
1 teaspoon salt
1 teaspoon garlic powder
$\frac{1}{4}$ teaspoon ground red pepper
$\frac{1}{2}$ teaspoon black pepper
8 chicken thighs (about 3 pounds)
  Olive oil cooking spray

1. Preheat oven to 350°F.

2. Beat egg slightly with water in shallow bowl; set aside. Mix bread crumbs, salt, garlic powder, red pepper and black pepper in separate shallow bowl.

3. Dip chicken thighs into egg mixture; turn to coat. Transfer to bread crumb mixture; press lightly to coat one side of chicken. Turn; repeat to coat other side. (Repeat with bread crumb mixture as needed to thoroughly coat chicken thighs.) Place coated chicken, skin side up, on large baking sheet.

4. Lightly spray tops of coated chicken with cooking spray. Bake, uncovered, for about 50 to 60 minutes or until browned and cooked through (180°F).*                                    *Makes 4 servings*

*Do not turn chicken while baking.*

Variations: Substitute flavored bread crumbs for the plain bread crumbs, garlic powder, red pepper, salt and black pepper. Or, substitute your favorite dried herbs or spices for the garlic powder and red pepper; thyme, sage, oregano, or rosemary would be delicious, as would Cajun or Creole seasoning.

# Thyme-Scented Roast Brisket Dinner

1 beef brisket (4 to 5 pounds)
2 teaspoons dried thyme
1 teaspoon salt
$\frac{1}{2}$ teaspoon black pepper
4 cloves garlic, minced
2 large onions, thinly sliced
1 can (about 14 ounces) beef broth
2 pounds red potatoes, halved or quartered
1 pound baby carrots
2 tablespoons butter
2 tablespoons all-purpose flour

1. Preheat oven to 350°F.

2. Place brisket, fat side up, in large roasting pan; sprinkle with thyme, salt, pepper and garlic. Separate onion slices into rings; scatter over brisket. Pour broth over onions. Cover; roast 2 to 3 hours. Uncover; stir onions into drippings. Arrange potatoes and carrots around brisket. Cover; roast 45 minutes more or until brisket and vegetables are fork-tender.

3. Turn off oven. Transfer brisket to cutting board; tent with foil and let stand 10 minutes. Transfer vegetables with slotted spoon to ovenproof serving bowl; keep warm in oven. Strain pan juices into measuring cup; refrigerate 15 minutes or until fat rises to top. Spoon off fat.

4. Melt butter in medium saucepan over medium heat. Add flour; cook and stir 1 minute. Add 1 cup pan juices to flour mixture; cook 3 to 4 minutes, stirring constantly, until sauce thickens.

5. Carve brisket into thin slices across grain. Serve with warm vegetables and sauce.

*Makes 8 servings*

# Farm-Raised Catfish with Bacon and Horseradish

6 (4- to 5-ounce) farm-raised catfish fillets
2 tablespoons butter
$\frac{1}{4}$ cup chopped onion
1 (8-ounce) package cream cheese, softened
$\frac{1}{4}$ cup dry white wine
2 tablespoons prepared horseradish
1 tablespoon Dijon mustard
$\frac{1}{2}$ teaspoon salt
$\frac{1}{8}$ teaspoon black pepper
4 strips bacon, cooked crisp and crumbled
2 tablespoons finely chopped fresh parsley (optional)

1. Preheat oven to 350°F. Grease large baking dish. Arrange fillets in single layer in prepared dish.

2. Melt butter in small skillet over medium-high heat. Add onion; cook and stir until softened. Combine cream cheese, wine, horseradish, mustard, salt and pepper in small bowl; stir in onion. Pour this mixture over fish and top with crumbled bacon. Bake 30 minutes or until fish begins to flake when tested with fork. Garnish with parsley. Serve immediately.

*Makes 6 servings*

# Caribbean Honey-Spiced Chicken

$^{1}/_{4}$ **cup honey**
$^{1}/_{4}$ **cup fresh lemon juice**
  **2 teaspoons freshly grated lemon peel**
  **1 ripe mango, peeled and diced**
  **2 fresh jalapeño peppers, halved and seeded***
  **1 small onion, peeled and quartered**
  **2 teaspoons paprika**
  **2 teaspoons vegetable oil**
**1$^{1}/_{2}$ teaspoons garlic salt**
  $^{1}/_{2}$ **teaspoon ground cinnamon**
  $^{1}/_{2}$ **teaspoon fresh ground pepper**
  $^{1}/_{2}$ **teaspoon ground allspice**
  **4 boneless skinless chicken breast halves**
  **1 tablespoon vegetable oil**

*\*Jalapeño peppers can sting and irritate the skin, so wear rubber gloves when handling peppers and do not touch your eyes.*

In small bowl, combine honey, lemon juice and lemon peel; whisk until well blended. Remove $^{1}/_{4}$ cup of mixture to food processor container; set aside. Add mango to honey mixture remaining in bowl; toss to coat. Reserve in refrigerator.

Add jalapeños, onion, paprika, oil, garlic salt, cinnamon, pepper and allspice to honey mixture in food processor container. Process until very finely chopped, scraping down sides when necessary. Spread mixture evenly over both sides of chicken breasts. Spread oil in 13×9-inch baking pan. Arrange chicken breasts in pan.

Bake at 375°F for 25 to 30 minutes or until chicken is no longer pink in center. Remove chicken to serving platter; top with reserved mango mixture. *Makes 4 servings*

Favorite recipe from **National Honey Board**

# Mexican Steak Tacos

1 (3.5-ounce) boil-in-bag long-grain rice
1 tablespoon ORTEGA® Salsa, any variety
2 teaspoons ground cumin
1 teaspoon garlic powder
1 teaspoon ORTEGA Taco Sauce
$^1/_4$ teaspoon salt
1 pound sirloin steak
   Nonstick cooking spray
1 can (about 14 ounces) diced tomatoes
1 can (4 ounces) ORTEGA Diced Green Chiles
1 package (12) ORTEGA Taco Shells
12 lime wedges
   Sour cream (optional)

**COOK** rice. Combine salsa, cumin, garlic powder, taco sauce and salt. Rub mixture over both sides of steak.

**SPRAY** a broiler pan with cooking spray. Place steak on pan. Broil steak for 4 minutes on each side or until desired degree of doneness. Cut steak into thin slices.

**COMBINE** rice, tomatoes and chiles. Place mixture in shells.

**TOP** rice mixture with beef slices. Squeeze juice from limes over beef. Top with sour cream, if desired.                    *Makes 12 servings*

# Cornish Hens with Andouille Stuffing

**4 Cornish game hens (about 1¼ pounds each), thawed**
**6 tablespoons butter, divided**
**2 links (8 ounces) fully cooked andouille or chicken andouille**
  **sausage, chopped**
**1 cup chopped onion**
**½ cup thinly sliced celery**
**1¼ to 1½ cups water**
  **1 bag (8 ounces) herb stuffing mix**
  **1 teaspoon dried thyme**
  **1 teaspoon paprika or smoked paprika**
  **1 teaspoon garlic salt**
**¼ teaspoon black pepper**
  **1 cup cranberry chutney or whole-berry cranberry sauce**

1. Preheat oven to 375°F. Grease 1-quart casserole; set aside. Rinse hens with cold water inside and out; pat dry with paper towels.

2. Melt 2 tablespoons butter in large saucepan over medium heat. Add sausage, onion and celery; cook 8 to 10 minutes or until vegetables are tender and sausage is browned, stirring occasionally. Add water (use 1½ cups water for a moister stuffing); bring to a boil. Remove from heat; add stuffing mix and toss well to combine. Spoon ½ cup stuffing into each hen cavity. Place hens on rack in shallow roasting pan. Tie legs together, if desired. Place remaining stuffing in prepared casserole.

3. Melt remaining 4 tablespoons butter. Add thyme, paprika, garlic salt and pepper; mix well. Brush half of butter mixture over hens. Roast hens for 30 minutes. Bake remaining stuffing alongside hens for 25 minutes. Brush remaining butter mixture over hens. Roast 20 to 25 minutes more or until legs move easily in socket and internal temperature of thigh reaches 180°F. Serve hens and stuffing with cranberry chutney. *Makes 4 servings*

# Chipotle-Marinated Beef Flank Steak

**1 beef flank steak (about 1$\frac{1}{2}$ to 2 pounds) or beef top round steak, cut 1 inch thick (about 1$\frac{3}{4}$ pounds)**
**Salt**

Marinade

**$\frac{1}{3}$ cup fresh lime juice**
**$\frac{1}{4}$ cup chopped fresh cilantro**
**1 tablespoon packed brown sugar**
**2 teaspoons minced chipotle chilies in adobo sauce**
**2 tablespoons adobo sauce (from chilies)**
**2 cloves garlic, minced**
**1 teaspoon freshly grated lime peel**

1. Combine marinade ingredients in small bowl; mix well. Place beef steak and marinade in food-safe plastic bag; turn steak to coat. Close bag securely and marinate in refrigerator 6 hours or as long as overnight.

2. Remove steak from marinade; discard marinade. Place steak on grid over medium, ash-covered coals. Grill flank steak, uncovered, 17 to 21 minutes for medium rare to medium doneness (top round steak 16 to 18 minutes for medium-rare doneness; do not overcook), turning occasionally. Carve steak across the grain into thin slices. Season with salt, as desired.

*Makes 4 to 6 servings*

Tip: To broil, place steak on rack in broiler pan so surface of beef is 2 to 3 inches from heat. Broil flank steak 13 to 18 minutes for medium-rare to medium doneness (top round steak 17 to 18 minutes for medium rare doneness; do not overcook), turning once.

Prep and Cook Time: **30 minutes**
Marinate Time: **6 hours or overnight**
Favorite recipe from **National Cattlemen's Beef Association on Behalf of The Beef Checkoff**

# Indian-Inspired Chicken with Raita

1 cup plain yogurt

2 cloves garlic, minced

1 teaspoon salt

1 teaspoon ground coriander

1 teaspoon ground ginger

$\frac{1}{2}$ teaspoon ground turmeric

$\frac{1}{2}$ teaspoon ground cinnamon

$\frac{1}{2}$ teaspoon ground cumin

$\frac{1}{4}$ teaspoon ground red pepper

1 (5- to 6-pound) chicken, cut into 8 pieces (about 4 pounds chicken parts)

Raita

2 medium cucumbers (about 1 pound), peeled, seeded and thinly sliced

$\frac{1}{3}$ cup plain yogurt

2 tablespoons chopped fresh cilantro

1 clove garlic, minced

$\frac{1}{4}$ teaspoon salt

$\frac{1}{8}$ teaspoon black pepper

1. Mix 1 cup yogurt, 2 cloves garlic, 1 teaspoon salt, coriander, ginger, turmeric, cinnamon, cumin and red pepper in large resealable food storage bag to blend. Add chicken; marinate in refrigerator 4 to 24 hours.

2. Preheat broiler. Cover baking sheet with foil. Place chicken on prepared baking sheet. Broil 6 inches from heat about 30 minutes or until cooked through, turning once.

3. Meanwhile, make Raita. Mix cucumbers, $\frac{1}{3}$ cup yogurt, cilantro, 1 clove garlic, $\frac{1}{4}$ teaspoon salt and black pepper in small bowl. Serve with chicken.

*Makes 6 to 8 servings*

# Veggie-Stuffed Portobello Mushrooms

4 large portobello mushrooms, about $1\frac{1}{4}$ to $1\frac{1}{2}$ pounds
  Nonstick cooking spray
2 teaspoons olive oil or butter
1 cup chopped green or red bell pepper
$\frac{1}{3}$ cup sliced shallots or chopped onion
2 cloves garlic, minced
1 cup chopped zucchini or summer squash
$\frac{1}{2}$ teaspoon salt
$\frac{1}{4}$ teaspoon black pepper
1 cup panko bread crumbs* or toasted fresh bread crumbs
1 cup shredded sharp Cheddar or mozzarella cheese

*Panko bread crumbs are light, crispy, Japanese-style bread crumbs. They can be found in the Asian food aisle of most supermarkets.*

1. Preheat broiler. Line baking sheet with foil. Gently remove mushroom stems; chop and set aside. Remove and discard brown gills from mushroom caps using spoon. Place mushroom caps right-side up on prepared baking sheet. Coat tops lightly with cooking spray. Broil 4 to 5 inches from heat 5 minutes or until tender.

2. Meanwhile, heat oil in large nonstick skillet over medium-high heat. Add bell pepper, shallots and garlic; cook 5 minutes or until bell peppers begin to brown on edges, stirring occasionally. Stir in zucchini, reserved chopped mushroom stems, salt and black pepper; cook 3 to 4 minutes or until vegetables are tender, stirring frequently. Remove from heat; cool 5 minutes. Stir in bread crumbs and cheese.

3. Turn mushroom caps over. Mound vegetable mixture into caps. Return to broiler; cook 2 to 3 minutes or until golden brown and cheese is melted.

*Makes 4 servings*

# Surf & Turf Kabobs

1 pound beef tenderloin, cut into 1¼-inch chunks
12 jumbo raw shrimp, peeled and deveined (with tails on)
1 medium onion, cut into 12 wedges
1 red or yellow bell pepper, cut into 1-inch chunks
⅓ cup butter, melted
3 tablespoons lemon juice
3 cloves garlic, minced
2 teaspoons paprika or smoked paprika
¼ teaspoon black pepper or ground red pepper
Lemon wedges

1. Spray grid with nonstick cooking spray. Prepare grill for direct cooking. Alternately thread beef, shrimp, onion and bell pepper onto 12-inch-long metal skewers. (Skewer shrimp through ends to form "C" shape for even cooking.)

2. Combine butter, lemon juice, garlic, paprika and black pepper in small bowl.

3. Place skewers on grid over medium coals; brush with half of butter mixture. Grill 5 minutes; turn and brush with remaining butter mixture. Continue grilling 5 to 6 minutes or until shrimp are pink and opaque (beef will be medium-rare to medium doneness). Serve with lemon wedges.

*Makes 4 servings*

# Greek-Style Braised Lamb Chops

1 teaspoon Greek seasoning
4 lamb shoulder chops (about 2$\frac{1}{2}$ pounds)
3 tablespoons olive oil
1 large onion, halved and sliced
1 bottle (12 ounces) beer
3 plum tomatoes, each cut into 6 wedges
$\frac{1}{2}$ cup pitted kalamata olives
1 tablespoon chopped fresh parsley

1. Rub Greek seasoning into chops. Set aside.

2. Heat oil over medium-high heat in large saucepan or Dutch oven. Cooking in 2 batches, add chops and brown on all sides. Remove chops to plate. Add onion; cook until soft. Pour in beer. Bring to boil over high heat, scraping bottom with wooden spoon to loosen browned bits. Reduce heat to medium; add lamb, tomatoes and olives. Cover and simmer over low heat 1 hour or until tender.

3. Remove chops to serving platter. Remove vegetables and olives to platter using slotted spoon. Tent with foil to keep warm. Bring remaining liquid to a boil over high heat. Reduce to about 1 cup. Pour sauce over chops and vegetables; sprinkle with parsley. *Makes 4 servings*

# Cavemen Beef Back Ribs

¼ **cup paprika**
¼ **cup brown sugar**
¼ **cup seasoned salt**
 2 **full racks beef back ribs, split in half (about 6 to 8 pounds)**
 1 **cup** *Cattlemen's®* **Authentic Smoke House Barbecue Sauce**
¼ **cup apple, pineapple or orange juice**

1. Combine paprika, sugar and seasoned salt. Rub mixture into ribs. Cover ribs and refrigerate 1 to 3 hours.

2. Prepare grill for indirect cooking over medium-low heat (250°F). Place ribs on rib rack or in foil pan. Cook on covered grill 2½ to 3 hours until very tender.

3. Meanwhile, combine barbecue sauce and juice. Brush mixture on ribs during last 30 minutes of cooking. Serve with additional barbecue sauce.

*Makes 6 to 8 servings*

Prep Time: 5 minutes
Cook Time: 3 hours
Marinate Time: 1 hour

For very tender ribs, remove membrane from underside of ribs before cooking. With a sharp paring knife, score membrane on bone from underside of ribs. Lift up portions of membrane with point of knife. Using kitchen towel, pull membrane away from bone and discard.

Main Attractions

# Santa Fe Fish Fillets with Mango-Cilantro Salsa

Nonstick cooking spray
1$\frac{1}{2}$ pounds fish fillets (cod, perch or tilapia, about $\frac{1}{2}$-inch thick)
$\frac{1}{2}$ package (3 tablespoons) ORTEGA® Taco Seasoning Mix
3 ORTEGA Taco Shells, finely crushed
1 cup ORTEGA Salsa, any variety
$\frac{1}{2}$ cup diced mango
2 tablespoons chopped cilantro

**PREHEAT** oven to 375°F. Cover broiler pan with foil. Spray with cooking spray.

**DIP** fish fillets in taco seasoning mix, coating both sides; place on foil. Spray coated fillets with cooking spray. Sprinkle with crushed taco shells.

**BAKE** 15 to 20 minutes until flaky in center.

**MICROWAVE** salsa on HIGH (100%) 1 minute. Stir in mango and cilantro.

**SPOON** salsa over fish before serving.                    *Makes 4 to 6 servings*

Note: Refrigerated jars of sliced mango can be found in the produce section at most supermarkets.

# Cocoa Spiced Beef Stir-Fry

2 cups beef broth
3 tablespoons soy sauce
2 tablespoons cornstarch
2 tablespoons HERSHEY'S Cocoa
2 teaspoons minced garlic (about 4 cloves)
1½ teaspoons ground ginger
1 teaspoon crushed red pepper flakes
1 pound boneless beef top round or flank steak
3 tablespoons vegetable oil, divided
1½ cups large onion pieces
1 cup carrot slices
3 cups fresh broccoli florets and pieces
1½ cups sweet red pepper slices
Hot cooked rice
Additional soy sauce
Cashew or peanut pieces (optional)

1. Stir together beef broth, soy sauce, cornstarch, cocoa, garlic, ginger and red pepper flakes; set aside. Cut beef steak into ¼-inch-wide strips.

2. Heat large skillet or wok over high heat about 1 minute or until hot. Drizzle about 1 tablespoon oil into pan; heat about 30 seconds. Add beef strips; stir-fry until well browned. Remove from heat; set aside.

3. Drizzle remaining 2 tablespoons oil into pan; add onion pieces and carrots. Stir-fry until onion is crisp, but tender. Add broccoli and red pepper strips; cook until crisp-tender.

4. Return beef to pan; add broth mixture. Cook and stir until mixture comes to a boil and thickens. Serve over hot rice with additional soy sauce and cashew pieces, if desired. *Makes 4 to 6 servings*

# Peach-Glazed Duck Breasts with Creole Rice

  2 tablespoons olive oil
$^1/_2$ cup *each* chopped onion and chopped celery
  3 cloves garlic, minced
  1 cup long-grain white rice or basmati rice
  1 can (about 14 ounces) chicken broth
  1 teaspoon blackened redfish seasoning mix, plus more to taste
  4 boneless duck breasts (6 to 7 ounces each) with skin
  1 teaspoon dried thyme
$^1/_4$ teaspoon *each* salt and black pepper
$^1/_3$ cup peach preserves
$1^1/_2$ tablespoons bourbon or whiskey

1. Heat oil in large skillet over medium heat. Add onion, celery and garlic; cook 5 minutes, stirring occasionally, until onion is translucent. Add rice; cook and stir 30 seconds. Stir in broth and seasoning mix. Reduce heat; cover and simmer 18 minutes or until liquid is absorbed.

2. Meanwhile, preheat oven to 350°F. Score skin of duck breasts with knife in crisscross fashion. Do not cut through to duck meat. Heat ovenproof skillet over medium heat. Place duck in skillet skin-side down. Sprinkle with thyme, salt and pepper. Cook 9 to 10 minutes or until skin is crispy and golden brown. Turn and cook 3 minutes more. Pour off drippings.

3. Combine preserves and bourbon in small bowl; spoon over duck. Transfer skillet to oven. Bake 12 to 14 minutes or until internal temperature reaches 155°F (or 8 to 10 minutes for medium rare). Transfer duck to cutting board; tent with foil and let stand 5 minutes. (Internal temperature of duck will rise by about 5°F). Place skillet with drippings over medium heat; simmer peach sauce in skillet 2 to 3 minutes or until thickened.

4. Spoon rice onto 4 serving plates. Carve duck crosswise into thin slices; arrange over rice. Spoon sauce over duck. *Makes 4 servings*

# Roasted Almond Tilapia

**2 tilapia fillets (6 ounces each) or Boston scrod fish fillets**
**¼ teaspoon salt**
**1 tablespoon coarse grain mustard**
**¼ cup whole wheat bread crumbs**
**2 tablespoons chopped unblanched almonds**
   **Paprika (optional)**
   **Lemon wedges**

1. Preheat oven to 450°F. Place fish on small baking sheet. Season with salt. Spread mustard over fish. Combine bread crumbs and almonds. Sprinkle over fish. Sprinkle paprika over fish, if desired.

2. Bake 8 to 10 minutes or until fish is opaque in center and begins to flake when tested with fork. Serve with lemon wedges.    *Makes 2 servings*

You can find fresh fish at most large supermarkets or at a retail fish markets. An independent retail fish market usually buys its fish on a daily basis, whereas chain stores order in large quantities and often do not receive daily shipments.

# Soups &
## sandwiches

# Pork Tenderloin Sliders

2 tablespoons olive oil, divided
2 pork tenderloins (about 1 pound each)
2 teaspoons chili powder
$^3/_4$ teaspoon ground cumin
$^1/_2$ teaspoon salt
$^1/_2$ teaspoon black pepper
12 green onions, ends trimmed
$^1/_2$ cup mayonnaise
1 chipotle pepper in adobo sauce, minced
2 teaspoons lime juice
12 dinner rolls, sliced in half horizontally
12 slices Monterey Jack cheese

1. Prepare grill for direct cooking.

2. Rub 1 tablespoon oil evenly over tenderloins. Combine chili powder, cumin, salt and black pepper in small bowl. Sprinkle evenly over tenderloins, coating all sides of meat. Place green onions and remaining 1 tablespoon oil in large resealable food storage bag; seal bag. Knead to coat green onions with oil; set aside.

3. Combine mayonnaise, chipotle pepper and lime juice is small bowl until well blended. Cover and refrigerate.

4. Grill tenderloins on covered grill 15 to 20 minutes or until internal temperature reaches 160°F, turning occasionally. Remove to cutting board. Tent with foil; let stand 10 minutes.

5. Meanwhile, grill green onions 3 minutes or until brown, turning frequently.

6. Coarsely chop grilled green onions. Thinly slice tenderloins. Evenly spread chipotle mayonnaise on bottom halves of rolls. Top with green onions, tenderloin slices and 1 slice cheese. Replace roll tops. Serve immediately. *Makes 6 sandwiches*

# Roasted Tomato Vegetable Soup

2 pounds grape or cherry tomatoes, stems removed

1 small onion, peeled, quartered

$1/4$ cup extra-virgin olive oil

$1/2$ teaspoon kosher salt

$1/4$ teaspoon black pepper

1 jar (12 ounces) roasted red peppers, drained

2 cans (15 ounces each) VEG•ALL® Original Mixed Vegetables,
   drained, with liquid reserved

1 cup water

5 to 6 leaves fresh basil

1 bay leaf

Preheat oven to 400°F.

Combine the first 5 ingredients in a Dutch oven. Toss to coat. Roast in oven 45 minutes. Remove from oven and let cool for 10 minutes.

Transfer tomato mixture, roasted peppers, Veg•All liquid, water and basil to a blender. Blend until smooth. Return soup to Dutch oven.

Add bay leaf and drained Veg•All vegetables. Simmer for 15 to 20 minutes over medium heat. Remove bay leaf. Ladle into bowls and serve.

*Makes 8 servings*

Serving Suggestion: Top each bowl of soup with croutons and crumbled gorgonzola cheese.

Soups & Sandwiches

# Quick Hot and Sour Chicken Soup

2 cups chicken broth

2 cups water

1 package (about 10 ounces) refrigerated fully-cooked
chicken breast strips, cut into pieces

1 package (about 7 ounces) chicken-flavored rice and
vermicelli mix

1 jalapeño pepper,* minced

2 green onions, chopped

1 tablespoon soy sauce

1 tablespoon lime juice

1 tablespoon minced fresh cilantro

*Jalapeño peppers can sting and irritate the skin, so wear rubber gloves when
handling peppers and do not touch your eyes.

1. Combine broth, water, chicken, rice mix, jalapeño pepper, green onions
and soy sauce in large saucepan. Bring to a boil over high heat. Reduce
heat to low. Cover; simmer 20 minutes or until rice is tender, stirring
occasionally.

2. Stir in lime juice; sprinkle with cilantro. *Makes 4 servings*

# Cuban Sandwiches

6 tablespoons *French's*® Classic Yellow® Mustard or
   *French's*® Sweet 'n Zesty Mustard
4 Kaiser rolls, split in half
8 ounces thinly sliced ham
8 ounces thinly sliced deli roast pork
8 ounces sandwich-style dill pickles
4 ounces thinly sliced Swiss or Muenster cheese

1. Spread mustard on cut sides of rolls. Layer ham, pork, pickles and cheese on bottoms of rolls. Cover with top halves of rolls. With bottom of a heavy skillet, press sandwiches firmly down on work surface to compress bread and filling.

2. Preheat an electric grill pan for 5 minutes. Place sandwiches on pan and close cover. Cook 6 minutes, turning halfway during cooking. Cut in half and serve hot.                                     *Makes 4 sandwiches*

Prep Time: **15 minutes**
Cook Time: **6 minutes**

If you don't have an electric grill pan, you can use a nonstick skillet to cook these sandwiches. Place a heavy skillet on top of the sandwiches to help flatten them during cooking.

# Spicy Meatball Sandwiches

1 large (17×15-inch) foil cooking bag
1 jar (26 ounces) marinara sauce
1 pound frozen pre-cooked Italian-style meatballs
$\frac{1}{2}$ cup chopped green bell pepper
$\frac{1}{3}$ cup sliced black olives
2 teaspoons Italian seasoning
$\frac{1}{4}$ teaspoon ground red pepper
6 slices mozzarella cheese, halved lengthwise
6 hoagie buns
3 tablespoons finely shredded Parmesan cheese

1. Prepare grill for direct cooking.

2. Place bag on baking sheet. Combine marinara sauce, meatballs, bell pepper, olives, Italian seasoning and red pepper in large bowl. Pour into bag. Double fold open side of bag, leaving head space for heat circulation.

3. Slide bag off baking sheet onto grill grid. Grill, covered, over medium-high coals 11 to 13 minutes or until meatballs are hot.

4. Meanwhile, place two pieces cheese on bottom of each bun. Carefully open bag to allow steam to escape. Spoon meatball mixture onto buns. Sprinkle with Parmesan cheese.  *Makes 6 sandwiches*

# Way-Long Sandwich

$^1/_2$ to $^3/_4$ cup mayonnaise
1$^1/_2$ teaspoons dried tarragon
1 clove minced garlic
$^1/_4$ teaspoon salt
1 loaf (16 ounces) Italian or French bread, cut in half lengthwise
2 medium tomatoes, thinly sliced
$^1/_4$ to $^1/_2$ cup thinly sliced red onion
2 cups chopped romaine lettuce
6 ounces thinly sliced deli roast beef
6 ounces thinly sliced deli smoked turkey
6 ounces sliced smoked provolone or Monterey Jack cheese with hot peppers

1. Combine mayonnaise, tarragon, garlic and salt in small bowl; stir until well blended.

2. Spread mayonnaise mixture evenly over cut sides of bread halves.

3. Layer bottom half of bread with tomatoes, onion, lettuce, roast beef, turkey and cheese. Cover with top half of bread; press down gently. Slice diagonally into 4 or 6 sandwiches.

*Makes 4 large or 6 regular sandwiches*

# Oxtail Soup with Beer

2½ pounds oxtails (may substitute beef or veal)
1 large onion, sliced
2 carrots, cut into 1-inch chunks
1 stalk celery, cut into 1-inch chunks
2 sprigs fresh parsley
5 peppercorns
1 bay leaf
4 cups beef broth
8 ounces dark beer
2 celery stalks, sliced
2 carrots, sliced
2 cups diced baking potatoes
1 teaspoon salt
2 tablespoons chopped fresh parsley (optional)

1. Combine oxtails, onion, carrot chunks, celery chunks, parsley sprigs, peppercorns and bay leaf in large saucepan. Pour beef broth and beer over mixture. Bring mixture to boil. Reduce to simmer, cover and cook over low heat 3 hours or until tender.

2. Remove oxtails; set aside. Strain broth and return to pan. Skim off excess fat. Add celery slices, carrot slices and potatoes; bring to simmer. Cook until just tender.

3. Discard connective tissue and fat from oxtails. Return meat to pan. Stir in salt. Ladle soup into bowls and garnish with chopped parsley.

*Makes 4 servings*

# Stuffed Focaccia Sandwich

1 container (about 5 ounces) soft cheese with garlic and herbs
1 (10-inch) round herb or onion focaccia, cut in half horizontally
$\frac{1}{2}$ cup thinly sliced red onion
$\frac{1}{2}$ cup coarsely chopped pimiento-stuffed green olives, drained
$\frac{1}{4}$ cup sliced mild banana pepper
4 ounces thinly sliced deli hard salami
6 ounces thinly sliced oven-roasted turkey breast
1 package ($\frac{2}{3}$ ounce) fresh basil, stems removed

1. Spread soft cheese over cut sides of focaccia. Layer bottom half evenly with onion, olives, banana pepper, salami, turkey and basil. Cover sandwich with top half of focaccia; press down firmly.

2. Cut sandwich into 4 equal pieces. Serve immediately or wrap individually in plastic wrap and refrigerate until serving time.          *Makes 4 sandwiches*

# Potato Chicken Soup

2$\frac{1}{2}$ pounds DOLE® Red Potatoes, peeled, cut into 1-inch cubes
$\frac{1}{2}$ pound DOLE® Peeled Mini Carrots, halved
1 container (32 ounces) chicken broth
$\frac{1}{2}$ bay leaf
2 teaspoons olive oil
1 small onion, cut into 1-inch cubes
1 teaspoon dried tarragon leaves, crushed
$\frac{1}{4}$ teaspoon dried thyme leaves, crushed
1$\frac{1}{2}$ cups cooked diced chicken
1 to 2 tablespoons minced parsley
$\frac{1}{8}$ teaspoon salt

• Combine potatoes, carrots, chicken broth and bay leaf in large pot. Bring to boil; reduce heat and simmer 15 to 20 minutes.

• Heat oil in nonstick skillet. Add onion; cook 6 to 8 minutes or until lightly browned. Add tarragon and thyme; cook 30 seconds.

• Add onion mixture, chicken, parsley and salt to soup in pot. Cook 5 minutes longer or until heated through. Remove bay leaf before serving.

*Makes 4 servings*

Prep Time: **25 minutes**
Cook Time: **35 minutes**

# Philly Cheesesteak Sandwiches

1 box (1 pound 5 ounces) frozen thin beef sandwich steaks
1 tablespoon olive oil
2 large sweet onions, halved and thinly sliced
1 large red bell pepper, cut into $1/4$-inch strips
$1/4$ teaspoon salt
$1/8$ teaspoon ground black pepper
1 jar (1 pound) RAGÚ® Cheesy! Double Cheddar Sauce
4 hoagie rolls, split

1. In 12-inch nonstick skillet, cook steaks, 2 at a time, over medium-high heat, stirring occasionally and breaking into pieces, 2 minutes or until done. Remove from skillet; set aside and keep warm. Repeat with remaining steaks. Clean skillet.

2. In same skillet, heat olive oil over medium heat and cook onions and red pepper, stirring occasionally, 15 minutes or until onions are caramelized. Season with salt and pepper.

3. Return steaks to skillet with half of the Double Cheddar Sauce. Cook, stirring occasionally, 2 minutes or until heated through.

4. To serve, evenly divide steak mixture on rolls, then drizzle with remaining Double Cheddar Sauce, heated.

*Makes 4 sandwiches*

Prep Time: **10 minutes**
Cook Time: **25 minutes**

# Chilled Cherry Soup

1 (1-pound) bag frozen pitted cherries
2 cups pinot noir
1 teaspoon grated lemon peel
$^1/_4$ cup sugar
$^1/_4$ cup honey
   Cinnamon stick
$^3/_4$ cup water, divided
   Dash salt and black pepper
2 tablespoons cornstarch
   Lemon or cherry sorbet (optional)

1. Combine cherries, pinot noir, lemon peel, sugar, honey, cinnamon stick, $^1/_2$ cup water, salt and pepper in large saucepan over medium heat. Stir to dissolve sugar and honey. Bring to a boil; reduce heat and simmer 15 minutes or until liquid is slightly reduced.

2. Combine cornstarch and remaining $^1/_4$ cup water in small bowl. Whisk cornstarch mixture into cherry mixture; return to a boil. Reduce heat and simmer 10 minutes or until slightly thickened.

3. Remove soup from heat. Remove and discard cinnamon stick. Place fine-meshed strainer over large bowl. Purée soup in blender, 1 cup at a time until smooth. Strain using rubber spatula or back of spoon to press out liquid. Chill completely. Serve soup with scoop of lemon sorbet, if desired.                    *Makes 4 servings*

Soups & Sandwiches

# Grilled Cobb Salad Sandwiches

$^1/_2$ medium avocado

1 green onion, chopped

$^1/_2$ teaspoon lemon juice

   Salt and black pepper

2 kaiser rolls, split

4 ounces thinly sliced deli chicken or turkey

4 slices cooked bacon

1 hard-cooked egg, sliced

2 slices (1 ounce each) Cheddar cheese

2 ounces blue cheese

   Tomato slices (optional)

   Olive oil

1. Mash avocado in small bowl; stir in green onion and lemon juice. Season with salt and pepper. Spread avocado mixture on top of rolls. Layer bottom of roll with chicken, bacon, egg, cheeses and tomato slices, if desired. Close sandwiches. Brush outsides of sandwiches lightly with oil.

2. Heat large nonstick skillet over medium heat. Add sandwiches; cook 4 to 5 minutes per side or until cheese melts and sandwiches are golden brown.

*Makes 2 sandwiches*

# Black & White Mexican Bean Soup

1 tablespoon vegetable oil
1 cup chopped onion
1 clove garlic, minced
¼ cup flour
1 package (1.25 ounces) ORTEGA® Taco Seasoning Mix
2 cups milk
1 can (about 14 ounces) chicken broth
1 package (16 ounces) frozen corn
1 can (about 15 ounces) great northern beans, rinsed and drained
1 can (about 15 ounces) black beans, rinsed and drained
1 can (4 ounces) ORTEGA Diced Green Chiles
2 tablespoons chopped cilantro

**HEAT** oil in large pan or Dutch oven over medium-high heat. Add onion and garlic; cook until onion is tender.

**STIR** in flour and taco seasoning mix; gradually stir in milk until blended. Add remaining ingredients except cilantro.

**BRING** to a boil, stirring constantly. Reduce heat to low; simmer for 15 minutes or until thickened, stirring occasionally.

**STIR** in cilantro.                          *Makes 6 servings*

# Open-Face Chicken Sandwiches with Roasted Pepper Mayo

4 boneless skinless chicken breasts (about $1/4$ pound each)
1 teaspoon dried thyme
1 teaspoon garlic salt
$1/4$ teaspoon black pepper
1 teaspoon olive oil or butter
$1/4$ cup mayonnaise
1 jar (2 ounces) diced pimiento, drained *or* 3 tablespoons chopped
   roasted red bell pepper
4 slices multi-grain, rye or sourdough bread, lightly toasted
1 cup packed watercress sprigs or baby spinach leaves

1. Place chicken between 2 sheets waxed paper or plastic wrap; pound to $1/3$-inch thickness. Sprinkle thyme, garlic salt and black pepper over chicken.

2. Heat oil in large nonstick skillet over medium heat. Add chicken; cook 4 to 5 minutes per side or until no longer pink in center.

3. Meanwhile, combine mayonnaise and pimiento in small bowl until well blended. Spread each toast slice with about $1 1/2$ teaspoons mayonnaise mixture. Place $1/4$ cup watercress on each slice of toast. Top each with chicken breast half and another $1 1/2$ teaspoons mayonnaise mixture.

*Makes 4 sandwiches*

# Thick and Creamy Succotash Soup

2 strips bacon
1 small onion, chopped
1 stalk celery, chopped
2 tablespoons all-purpose flour
3 cups chicken broth
1$\frac{1}{2}$ cups fresh or frozen corn
1 cup frozen baby lima beans, thawed
1 bay leaf
$\frac{1}{4}$ teaspoon salt
$\frac{1}{4}$ teaspoon black pepper
$\frac{1}{4}$ teaspoon hot pepper sauce
$\frac{1}{2}$ cup whipping cream

1. Cook bacon in Dutch oven over medium heat until crisp and browned. Drain on paper towel. Crumble and set aside.

2. Add onion and celery to bacon drippings in Dutch oven; cook and stir 5 minutes or until tender. Stir in flour; cook 1 to 2 minutes. Stir in chicken broth. Bring to a boil; cook and stir until slightly thickened.

3. Add bacon, corn, beans, bay leaf, salt, black pepper and hot pepper sauce. Reduce heat to low. Simmer 15 minutes. Stir in cream. Remove from heat. Remove bay leaf before serving.

*Makes 6 servings*

Tip: This soup can be covered and refrigerated up to one day. Reheat over low heat. (Do not allow soup to boil.)

# Havarti & Onion Sandwiches

1½ teaspoons olive oil

⅓ cup thinly sliced red onion

4 slices pumpernickel bread

6 ounces dill havarti cheese, cut into slices

½ cup prepared coleslaw

1. Heat oil in large nonstick skillet over medium heat. Add onion; cook and stir 5 minutes or until tender. Layer 2 bread slices with onion, cheese and coleslaw; top with remaining 2 bread slices.

2. Heat same skillet over medium heat. Add sandwiches; press down with spatula. Cook sandwiches 4 to 5 minutes per side or until cheese melts and sandwiches are toasted. *Makes 2 sandwiches*

Havarti cheese is a semisoft cheese that is pale yellow and has nonuniform holes in it. The flavor of young havarti cheese is mild, yet tangy, while aged havarti has those flavors intensified and sharpened. This cheese is often found in loaves or blocks and is sometimes found wrapped in foil.

# Vegetable and Red Lentil Soup

1 can (about 14 ounces) vegetable broth
1 can (about 14 ounces) diced tomatoes
2 medium zucchini or yellow summer squash (or 1 of each), diced
1 red or yellow bell pepper, diced
$\frac{1}{2}$ cup thinly sliced carrots
$\frac{1}{2}$ cup red lentils, rinsed and sorted*
$\frac{1}{2}$ teaspoon salt
$\frac{1}{2}$ teaspoon sugar
$\frac{1}{4}$ teaspoon black pepper
2 tablespoons chopped fresh basil or thyme
$\frac{1}{2}$ cup croutons or shredded cheese (optional)

*If you have difficulty finding red lentils, substitute brown lentils.

**Slow Cooker Directions**

1. Combine broth, tomatoes, zucchini, bell pepper, carrots, lentils, salt, sugar and black pepper in slow cooker; mix well. Cover; cook on LOW 8 hours or on HIGH 4 hours.

2. Ladle into shallow bowls; top with basil and croutons, if desired.

*Makes 4 servings*

# Rustic Grilled Chicken Sandwich

1 pound boneless skinless chicken breasts, thinly sliced

¾ cup *French's® Gourmayo™* Creamy Dijon Flavored Light Mayonnaise or *French's® Gourmayo™* Caesar Ranch Flavored Light Mayonnaise

3 tablespoons lemon juice

3 tablespoons minced fresh herbs (parsley, basil, thyme or any combination)

1 loaf artisan or rustic-style bread, split in half (remove excess dough from insides)

2 cups mixed field greens or baby spinach

1 (7-ounce) jar sun-dried tomatoes packed in oil, drained and cut into slivers

1. Place chicken into resealable plastic food storage bag. Combine mayonnaise, lemon juice and herbs. Pour ¾ cup mixture over chicken in bag. Seal bag; shake chicken to coat evenly. Marinate in refrigerator 30 minutes or up to 1 hour.

2. Grill or broil chicken 5 to 8 minutes until no longer pink in center.

3. Spread remaining mayonnaise mixture on both sides of bread. Layer field greens and tomatoes on bottom half of bread. Top with chicken pieces and cover with top half of bread. Cut into quarters to serve.

*Makes 4 sandwiches*

Prep Time: **10 minutes**
Cook Time: **8 minutes**
Marinate Time: **30 minutes**

# Cream of Broccoli Soup with Croutons

Croutons

    3 cups French or rustic bread, cut into $\frac{1}{2}$-inch cubes

    1 tablespoon butter, melted

    1 tablespoon olive oil

    $\frac{1}{4}$ cup grated Parmesan cheese

Soup

    2 tablespoons butter

    1 large onion, chopped

    8 cups chopped broccoli (about $1\frac{1}{2}$ pounds)

    3 cups chicken broth

    1 cup whipping cream or half-and-half

  $1\frac{1}{2}$ teaspoons salt

    $\frac{1}{2}$ teaspoon black pepper

1. For croutons, preheat oven to 350°F. Toss bread cubes with 1 tablespoon melted butter and oil. Add cheese; toss again and transfer to 15×10-inch jelly-roll pan. Bake 12 to 14 minutes or until golden brown, stirring after 8 minutes. Cool completely. Transfer to airtight container. (May be prepared up to 2 days before serving.)

2. For soup, melt 2 tablespoons butter in large saucepan over medium heat. Add onion; cook 5 minutes, stirring occasionally. Add broccoli and broth to onion mixture. Cover and bring to a boil over high heat. Reduce heat; simmer 25 minutes or until very tender. Cool 10 minutes.

3. Transfer in batches to blender or food processor; blend until smooth and return to saucepan. Stir in cream, salt and pepper; warm until heated through. (Do not allow soup to boil.) Ladle into bowls and top with croutons.

*Makes 8 servings*

Note: Soup may be cooled and refrigerated up to 2 days before serving.

# Grilled Cuban Party Sandwich

$^3/_4$ cup plus 1 to 2 tablespoons olive oil, divided

6 tablespoons lime juice

4 cloves garlic, minced

Salt and black pepper

2 boneless skinless chicken breasts (about $^1/_2$ pound)

1 medium yellow onion, cut into $^1/_2$-inch thick slices

1 loaf ciabatta bread (1 pound), cut in half lengthwise

$^1/_4$ cup chopped fresh cilantro

6 ounces fresh mozzarella, sliced

1 medium tomato, thinly sliced

1. Combine $^3/_4$ cup oil, lime juice, garlic, salt and pepper in medium bowl; mix well. Pour $^1/_4$ cup of marinade into resealable food storage bag; refrigerate remaining marinade. Add chicken to bag; seal. Coat well and refrigerate up to 2 hours.

2. Brush grid with small amount of oil. Prepare grill for direct cooking.

3. Remove chicken from marinade; discard marinade. Grill chicken 12 to 15 minutes on uncovered grill or until no longer pink in center, turning halfway through cooking. Thread onion onto skewers and brush with 1 tablespoon oil. Place on grill beside chicken. Grill 8 to 12 minutes or until soft and browned, turning halfway through cooking.

4. Let chicken stand 10 minutes. Meanwhile, season onions with salt and pepper and separate into rings. Toast bread on grill. Thinly slice chicken.

5. Stir reserved marinade and brush onto grilled bread. Sprinkle cilantro onto bottom half. Top with layers of cheese, tomato, chicken and seasoned onions. Top with remaining bread. Wrap sandwich in foil. Place on grill; top with large heavy skillet to flatten. Grill 4 to 6 minutes or until cheese melts. Cut into 6 pieces. Serve immediately. *Makes 6 sandwiches*

# Chicken Tortellini Soup

**6 cups chicken broth**

**1 package (9 ounces) refrigerated cheese and spinach tortellini or three-cheese tortellini**

**1 package (about 6 ounces) refrigerated fully-cooked chicken breast strips, cut into bite-size pieces**

**2 cups coarsely chopped baby spinach leaves**

**4 to 6 tablespoons grated Parmesan cheese**

**1 tablespoon chopped chives *or* 2 tablespoons sliced green onion**

1. Bring chicken broth to a boil in large saucepan over high heat. Add tortellini. Reduce heat to medium; cook 5 minutes. Stir in chicken and spinach.

2. Reduce heat to low; cook 3 minutes or until chicken is hot. Sprinkle with Parmesan cheese and chives. *Makes 4 servings*

# Pulled Turkey Sandwiches

1 tablespoon vegetable oil
1 small red onion, chopped
1 celery stalk, trimmed and chopped
3 cups cooked turkey thigh meat, cut into large chunks
1 can (8 ounces) tomato sauce
¼ cup ketchup
2 tablespoons packed brown sugar
1 tablespoon cider vinegar
2 teaspoons Worcestershire sauce
1 teaspoon Dijon mustard
¼ teaspoon chipotle chile powder
⅛ teaspoon salt
4 hamburger buns

1. Heat oil in Dutch oven or deep skillet over medium-high heat. Add onion and celery; cook and stir 5 minutes.

2. Stir in turkey, tomato sauce, ketchup, brown sugar, cider vinegar, Worcestershire sauce, mustard, chile powder and salt. Cover and simmer 45 minutes to 1 hour or until turkey shreds easily with fork.

3. Serve turkey in buns.                    *Makes 4 sandwiches*

*tip*

The pulled turkey in these sandwiches freezes very well. Try doubling the recipe and freezing any leftovers. Before serving, simply thaw the turkey in the refrigerator and reheat in the microwave.

# Cheesy Mexican Soup

1 cup chopped onion
1 tablespoon vegetable oil
2 cups milk
1 can (about 14 ounces) chicken broth
1 container (13 ounces) ORTEGA® Salsa & Cheese Bowl
1 can (7 ounces) ORTEGA Diced Green Chiles
4 ORTEGA Taco Shells, crushed
$\frac{1}{4}$ cup chopped cilantro

**COOK** and stir onion in oil in large saucepan over medium-high heat for 4 to 6 minutes until tender. Reduce heat to medium-low.

**STIR** in milk, chicken broth, Salsa & Cheese and green chiles; cook for 5 to 7 minutes until hot, stirring frequently.

**MICROWAVE** crushed taco shells on HIGH (100%) 30 to 45 seconds. Cool. Serve soup sprinkled with crushed taco shells and cilantro.

*Makes 8 servings*

# Sweet & Tasty Hawaiian Sandwich

$^1/_2$ cup pineapple preserves

1 tablespoon Dijon mustard

1 round loaf (16 ounces) Hawaiian bread

8 ounces brick cheese, thinly sliced

8 ounces thinly sliced deli ham

Olive oil

Pimiento-stuffed green olives (optional)

1. Combine preserves and mustard in small bowl; mix well. Cut bread in half horizontally. Pull out and discard center from bread top, leaving 1-inch shell. Spread preserves mixture on bottom half of bread. Layer with cheese and ham; close sandwich with top half of bread. Brush outsides of sandwich lightly with oil.

2. Heat large nonstick skillet over medium heat. Add sandwich; press down lightly with spatula or weigh down with small plate. Cook sandwich 4 to 5 minutes per side or until cheese melts and sandwich is golden brown. Cut into wedges; garnish with green olives. *Makes 4 to 6 servings*

# Hot and Sour Soup

1 package (1 ounce) dried shiitake mushrooms
4 ounces firm tofu, drained
4 cups chicken broth
3 tablespoons white vinegar
2 tablespoons soy sauce
$\frac{1}{2}$ to 1 teaspoon hot chili oil
$\frac{1}{4}$ teaspoon white pepper
1 cup shredded cooked pork, chicken or turkey
$\frac{1}{2}$ cup drained canned bamboo shoots, cut into thin strips
3 tablespoons water
2 tablespoons cornstarch
1 egg white, lightly beaten
$\frac{1}{4}$ cup thinly sliced green onions or chopped fresh cilantro
1 teaspoon dark sesame oil

1. Place mushrooms in small bowl; cover with warm water. Soak 20 minutes to soften. Drain; squeeze out excess water. Discard stems; slice caps. Press tofu lightly between paper towels; cut into $\frac{1}{2}$-inch squares or triangles.

2. Combine broth, vinegar, soy sauce, chili oil and white pepper in medium saucepan. Bring to a boil over high heat. Reduce heat to medium and simmer 2 minutes.

3. Stir in mushrooms, tofu, pork and bamboo shoots; heat through.

4. Blend water into cornstarch until smooth. Stir into soup. Cook and stir 4 minutes or until soup boils and thickens. Remove from heat.

5. Stirring constantly in one direction, slowly pour egg white in thin stream into soup. Stir in green onions and sesame oil. Ladle into soup bowls.

*Makes 4 to 6 servings*

# White Bean Soup

6 strips bacon, cut into $\frac{1}{2}$-inch pieces
3 cans (about 15 ounces each) white beans, rinsed and drained, divided
3 cans (about 14 ounces each) chicken broth
1 medium onion, finely chopped
3 cloves garlic, minced
$1\frac{1}{2}$ teaspoons dried thyme
$1\frac{1}{2}$ teaspoons dried rosemary

1. Cook and stir bacon in Dutch oven over medium-high heat about 10 minutes or until crisp.

2. Meanwhile, blend $1\frac{1}{2}$ cans beans and broth in blender or food processor until smooth.

3. Drain all but 1 tablespoon bacon fat from Dutch oven. Stir in onion, garlic, thyme and rosemary. Reduce heat to medium; cover and cook 3 minutes or until onion is transparent.

4. Add puréed bean mixture and remaining $1\frac{1}{2}$ cans beans to onion mixture. Cover and simmer 5 minutes or until heated through.

*Makes 4 servings*

Prep and Cook Time: **28 minutes**

# Barbecue Steak Sandwiches with Smothered Onions

1 tablespoon vegetable oil
8 to 12 slices (about 1 pound) minute steaks
1 large Vidalia or other sweet onion, sliced
$^3/_4$ cup CATTLEMEN'S® Authentic Smoke House Barbecue Sauce
$^1/_4$ cup *French's*® Worcestershire Sauce or *Frank's*® *RedHot*® Cayenne
    Pepper Sauce
8 slices Jack or American cheese
4 sub or hero rolls, split

1. Heat oil in large nonstick skillet until very hot. Cook steaks 5 minutes until browned, turning once; remove from skillet.

2. Sauté onion in same skillet until tender. Add barbecue sauce and Worcestershire. Heat through.

3. Spoon saucy onions on bottoms of rolls, dividing evenly. Arrange 2 or 3 pieces steak on each sandwich and top with 2 slices cheese. Close rolls.

*Makes 4 servings*

Prep Time: **5 minutes**
Cook Time: **10 minutes**

# Punch

*pizzazz*

# Guava Fruit Punch

1½ cups boiling water
2 tea bags
3 thin slices peeled fresh ginger
2 cups guava juice
¾ cup pineapple juice
1 to 2 tablespoons lemon juice
Ice cubes
Mint sprigs (optional)

**1.** Combine water, tea bags and ginger in heatproof pitcher; steep 5 minutes. Discard tea bags and ginger.

**2.** Add guava juice, pineapple juice and lemon juice to tea mixture; mix well. Serve in tall glasses over ice. Garnish with mint.          *Makes 4 servings*

Guava is an aromatic, sweet tropical fruit that grows in South America as well as in California, Florida and Hawaii. Most of the domestic crop is processed into juice, jellies and sauces. Fresh guavas are round or slightly oval in shape, two to three inches in diameter with several small, hard edible seeds.

# Raspberry Wine Punch

1 package (10 ounces) frozen red raspberries in syrup, thawed
1 bottle (750 mL) white Zinfandel or blush wine
$\frac{1}{4}$ cup raspberry-flavored liqueur
   Crushed ice
   Fresh raspberries (optional)

1. Process raspberries with syrup in food processor or blender until smooth. Press through strainer; discard seeds.

2. Combine wine, raspberry purée and liqueur in pitcher; refrigerate until serving time.

3. Serve in cocktail or wine glasses over crushed ice. Garnish with fresh raspberries. *Makes 8 servings*

# Quick Apple Punch

4 cups MOTT'S® Apple Juice
2 cups cranberry juice cocktail
2 tablespoons lemon juice
1 liter ginger ale, chilled
   Crushed ice, as needed

In large bowl, combine apple juice, cranberry juice and lemon juice. Fifteen minutes before serving, add ginger ale and crushed ice. Do not stir.

*Makes 15 servings*

# Warm & Spicy Fruit Punch

4 cinnamon sticks
   Juice and peel of 1 orange
1 teaspoon whole allspice
$\frac{1}{2}$ teaspoon whole cloves
7 cups water
1 can (12 ounces) frozen cranberry-raspberry juice concentrate, thawed
1 can (6 ounces) frozen lemonade concentrate, thawed
2 cans ($5\frac{1}{2}$ ounces each) apricot nectar

**Slow Cooker Directions**

1. Break cinnamon sticks into pieces. Tie cinnamon sticks, orange peel, allspice and cloves in cheesecloth bag.

2. Combine orange juice, water, concentrates and apricot nectar in slow cooker; add spice bag. Cover; cook on LOW 5 to 6 hours.

3. Remove and discard spice bag.     *Makes about 14 (6-ounce) servings*

Prep Time: **10 minutes**
Cook Time: **5 to 6 hours**

# Champagne Punch

1 orange
1 lemon
$\frac{1}{4}$ cup cranberry-flavored liqueur or cognac
$\frac{1}{4}$ cup orange-flavored liqueur or Triple Sec
1 bottle (750 mL) sparkling pink or white wine or champagne, well chilled
Fresh cranberries (optional)
Citrus strips (optional)

1. Remove colored peel, not white pith, from orange and lemon in long thin strips using citrus peeler. Refrigerate orange and lemon for another use. Combine peels and cranberry- and orange-flavored liqueurs in glass pitcher. Cover and refrigerate 2 to 6 hours.

2. Just before serving, tilt pitcher to one side and slowly pour in sparkling wine. Leave peels in pitcher for added flavor. Place cranberry in bottom of each champagne glass, if desired. Pour punch into glasses; garnish with citrus strips. *Makes 4 cups (6 to 8 servings)*

# Kahlúa® Party Punch

2 cups KAHLÚA® Liqueur
1 can (12 ounces) frozen apple juice concentrate, undiluted
1/2 cup lemon juice
1 small block of ice
1 bottle (25.4 ounces) sparkling apple juice
1 quart club soda or lemon-lime beverage
1 bottle (750 mL) dry champagne
Thin lemon slices and small orange slices for garnish

Refrigerate ingredients until well chilled. Combine Kahlúa® with apple juice concentrate and lemon juice. Pour over ice in punch bowl. Add sparkling apple juice, club soda and champagne; stir gently. Add lemon and orange slices. *Makes 30 (1/2-cup) servings (about 1 gallon)*

Note: Kahlúa®, apple juice concentrate and lemon juice may be mixed and refrigerated the day before.

# Hot Holiday Punch

4 cups apple cider
1 cup granulated sugar
$\frac{1}{2}$ cup packed brown sugar
1 cinnamon stick
12 whole cloves
2 cups Florida grapefruit juice
2 cups Florida orange juice
Florida orange slices
Maraschino cherry halves (optional)
Whole cloves (optional)

Combine apple cider and sugars in large saucepan. Heat over medium heat, stirring until sugars dissolve. Add cinnamon stick and cloves. Bring to a boil over medium heat. Reduce heat to low; simmer 5 minutes. Add grapefruit and orange juices. Heat, but do not boil. Strain into heatproof punch bowl. Garnish with orange slices decorated with maraschino cherry halves and whole cloves. Serve in heatproof punch cups.

*Makes 8 (8-ounce) servings*

Favorite recipe from **Florida Department of Citrus**

# Piña Colada Punch

5 cups DOLE® Pineapple Juice, divided
1 can (15 ounces) real cream of coconut
1 liter lemon-lime soda
2 limes
1½ cups light rum (optional)
   Ice cubes
   Fresh mint sprigs

• Chill all ingredients.

• Blend 2 cups pineapple juice and cream of coconut in blender. Combine puréed mixture with remaining 3 cups pineapple juice, soda, juice of 1 lime, rum and ice. Garnish with 1 sliced lime and mint sprigs.

*Makes 15 servings*

# Pineapple Raspberry Punch

5 cups DOLE® Pineapple Juice
1 quart raspberry cranberry drink
1 pint fresh or frozen raspberries
1 lemon, thinly sliced
   Ice cubes

• Chill ingredients. Combine in punch bowl.

*Makes 9 cups*

# Hot Cranberry-Lemon Wine Punch

3 cups water
$3/4$ to 1 cup sugar
20 whole cloves
2 sticks cinnamon
1 bottle (750 mL) rosé wine
1 bottle (32 ounces) cranberry juice cocktail
Juice of 6 SUNKIST® lemons (1 cup)

In saucepot, combine water, sugar and spices. Bring to boil, stirring until sugar dissolves. Reduce heat; simmer 5 minutes. Remove spices. Add remaining ingredients; heat. For garnish, float clove-studded lemon cartwheel slices in punch, if desired.

*Makes about 11 cups (18 (5-ounce) servings)*

Cold Cranberry-Lemon Wine Punch: After simmering water, sugar and spices, chill syrup mixture. To serve, in punch bowl combine all ingredients. Add $1/2$ cup brandy, if desired. Add ice or float an ice ring.

# Sparkling Apple Punch

2 bottles (750 mL each) sparkling apple cider, chilled
1½ quarts papaya or apricot nectar, chilled
    Ice
1 or 2 papayas, peeled and chopped
    Orange slices, quartered

Combine apple cider, papaya nectar and ice in punch bowl. Add papaya and orange slices.

*Makes about 4 quarts*

# Citrus Punch

4 oranges, cut into ⅛-inch slices
1 pint strawberries, stemmed and halved
1 to 2 limes, cut into ⅛-inch slices
1 lemon, cut into ⅛-inch slices
1 cup raspberries
2 cups *each* orange juice and grapefruit juice
¾ cup lime juice
½ cup light corn syrup
1 bottle (750 mL) ginger ale, white grape juice or sparkling wine
    Fresh mint sprigs (optional)

1. Spread oranges, strawberries, limes, lemon and raspberries on baking sheet. Freeze 4 hours or until firm.

2. Combine orange juice, grapefruit juice, lime juice and corn syrup in 2-quart pitcher. Stir until corn syrup dissolves. Refrigerate 2 hours or until cold. Stir in ginger ale just before serving.

3. Divide frozen fruit between 8 (12-ounce) glasses or 10 wide-rimmed wine glasses. Fill glasses with punch. Garnish with mint. Serve immediately.

*Makes 8 to 10 servings (about 5 cups)*

# "Lemon Float" Punch

Juice of 10 to 12 SUNKIST® lemons (2 cups)
¾ cup sugar
4 cups water
1 bottle (2 liters) ginger ale, chilled
1 pint lemon sherbet or frozen vanilla yogurt
Lemon half-cartwheel slices and fresh mint leaves for garnish

Combine lemon juice and sugar; stir to dissolve sugar. Add water; chill. To serve, in large punch bowl, combine lemon mixture and ginger ale. Add small scoops of sherbet, lemon slices and mint.

*Makes about 20 (6-ounce) servings*

Sherbet refers to a frozen dessert made from fruit, fruit juices, sugar, stabilizers and flavorings. In the United States, sherbet often contains milk solids. The French term is sorbet and the Italian term sorbetto, but neither contain milk products.

# Spiced Cranberry Punch

2 cups KARO® Light Corn Syrup
¹/₄ cup water
6 cinnamon sticks
2 tablespoons whole cloves
¹/₂ teaspoon ground allspice
2 quarts cranberry juice, chilled
1 quart orange juice, chilled
1 can (46 ounces) pineapple juice, chilled
2 quarts ginger ale, chilled
¹/₂ cup lemon juice

1. In medium saucepan, combine corn syrup, water, cinnamon sticks, cloves and allspice. Bring to boil over medium-high heat. Reduce heat; simmer 10 minutes.

2. Cover and refrigerate until thoroughly chilled; strain to remove spices.

3. Just before serving, add spiced syrup, fruit juices, ginger ale and lemon juice. *Makes about 36 (6-ounce) servings*

Prep Time: **15 minutes, plus chilling**

# Peaches and Cream Punch

4 cups boiling water
6 LIPTON® Brisk Regular or Decaffeinated Tea Bags
4 cans (12 ounces each) peach nectar, chilled
2 cups Champagne or seltzer, chilled
1 container (16 ounces) frozen vanilla lowfat yogurt

In teapot, pour boiling water over tea bags; cover and brew 5 minutes. Remove tea bags and cool.

In chilled 4-quart punch bowl, blend peach nectar with tea. Just before serving, add Champagne. Top with scoops of yogurt and garnish, if desired, with fresh peach slices. Serve immediately.

*Makes 24 (4-ounce) servings*

# Cranberry Snow Punch

1 cup apple juice, chilled
$1/2$ cup superfine sugar
$1^1/2$ cups cranberry juice cocktail, chilled
$1^1/2$ cups bitter lemon or tonic water, chilled
1 pint vanilla frozen yogurt

1. Combine apple juice and sugar in punch bowl; stir until sugar dissolves. Stir in cranberry juice and bitter lemon.

2. Scoop frozen yogurt onto top of punch. Serve immediately.

*Makes 8 servings (about 4 ounces each)*

# Pineapple-Champagne Punch

1 quart pineapple sherbet
1 quart unsweetened pineapple juice, chilled
1 bottle (750 mL) dry champagne, chilled
2 fresh or canned pineapple slices, each cut into 6 wedges
   Sliced strawberries (optional)
   Mint sprigs (optional)

**1.** Process sherbet and pineapple juice in blender until smooth and frothy. Pour into punch bowl. Stir in champagne.

**2.** Float pineapple slices in punch; garnish with strawberries and mint. Serve immediately.                *Makes 20 (4-ounce) servings*

# Golden Harvest Punch

4 cups MOTT'S® Apple Juice
4 cups orange juice
3 liters club soda
1 quart orange sherbet *or* 5 pound bag ice cubes

Combine apple juice, orange juice and club soda in punch bowl. Add scoops of sherbet.                        *Makes 25 servings*

# Holiday Citrus Punch

1 pint vanilla frozen yogurt, softened
Fresh or frozen raspberries
1 can (12 ounces) frozen lemonade concentrate, thawed
1 can (12 ounces) frozen orange-cranberry juice concentrate, thawed
1 can (12 ounces) frozen Ruby Red grapefruit juice concentrate, thawed
2 cups cold water
$\frac{1}{4}$ cup lime juice
2 bottles (28 ounces each) ginger ale, chilled

1. Line 9-inch square baking dish with parchment paper. Spread yogurt evenly in prepared dish; freeze until firm. Meanwhile, place baking sheet in freezer to chill.

2. Remove frozen yogurt from baking dish. Cut out desired shapes with assorted cookie cutters from frozen yogurt. Transfer cutouts to chilled baking sheet. Press raspberry into center of each yogurt cutout; freeze until ready to serve.

3. Combine lemonade and juice concentrates, water and lime juice in punch bowl. Just before serving, add ginger ale. Float yogurt cutouts in punch.

*Makes 24 to 26 servings*

# Warming Winter Punch

1 unpeeled SUNKIST® orange, cut into half-cartwheel slices
1 unpeeled SUNKIST® lemon, cut into half-cartwheel slices
2 cups water
$\frac{1}{2}$ cup packed brown sugar
4 cinnamon sticks
8 whole cloves
4 cups freshly squeezed SUNKIST® orange juice
2 cups pineapple juice
Juice of 2 SUNKIST® lemons

Place citrus slices in heat-proof bowl or large pitcher. In large saucepan, combine water, brown sugar, cinnamon and cloves; bring to a boil. Reduce heat and simmer, uncovered, 10 minutes. Add juices and heat. *Do not boil.* Pour over citrus slices; stir well.                    *Makes about 8 cups*

Tip: Also good chilled and served over ice.

# Cranberry-Lime Margarita Punch

6 cups water
1 can (12 ounces) frozen cranberry juice cocktail concentrate, thawed
$\frac{1}{2}$ cup lime juice
$\frac{1}{4}$ cup sugar
2 cups ice cubes
1 cup tequila
Fresh cranberries (optional)
1 lime, sliced (optional)

**1.** Combine water, juice concentrate and sugar in punch bowl; stir until sugar dissolves.

**2.** Stir in ice cubes and tequila. Garnish with cranberries and lime slices.

*Makes 10 (8-ounce) servings*

# Brandied Cranapple Punch

$1\frac{1}{2}$ quarts (6 cups) cranapple juice cocktail
1 small orange, thinly sliced
$\frac{1}{4}$ cup packed light brown sugar
3 cinnamon sticks
12 whole cloves
1 cup brandy or cognac
Additional orange slices (optional)

**1.** Combine juice cocktail, orange slices, brown sugar, cinnamon sticks and cloves in large saucepan. Bring to a simmer over medium heat. Reduce heat to low; add brandy.

**2.** Ladle into mugs, leaving cinnamon sticks and cloves in saucepan. Garnish with additional orange slices.

*Makes 6 to 8 servings*

# Strawberry Champagne Punch

2 packages (10 ounces each) frozen sliced strawberries in syrup, thawed
2 cans (5$\frac{1}{2}$ ounces each) apricot or peach nectar
$\frac{1}{4}$ cup lemon juice
2 tablespoons honey
2 bottles (750 mL each) champagne or sparkling white wine, chilled
Lemon slices (optional)
Fresh strawberry halves (optional)
Mint leaves (optional)

1. Place strawberries with syrup in food processor or blender; process until smooth.

2. Pour puréed strawberries into large punch bowl. Stir in apricot nectar, lemon juice and honey; blend well. Refrigerate until serving time.

3. To serve, stir champagne into strawberry mixture. Garnish with lemon slices, strawberry halves and mint. *Makes 12 servings*

Tip: To save time, thaw the strawberries in the refrigerator the day before using them.

Prep Time: **15 minutes**

# Piña Colada Punch

3 cups water

10 whole cloves

4 cardamom pods

2 sticks cinnamon

1 pint piña colada frozen yogurt, softened*

1 can (12 ounces) frozen pineapple juice concentrate, thawed

$1\frac{1}{4}$ cups lemon seltzer water

$1\frac{1}{4}$ teaspoons rum extract

$\frac{3}{4}$ teaspoon coconut extract (optional)

Mint sprigs (optional)

*Can substitute pineapple sherbet for piña colada frozen yogurt. When using pineapple sherbet, use coconut extract for a more authentic flavor.*

1. Combine water, cloves, cardamom and cinnamon in small saucepan. Bring to a boil over high heat; reduce heat to low. Simmer, covered, 5 minutes; cool. Strain spices; discard.

2. Combine spiced water, frozen yogurt and juice concentrate in small punch bowl or pitcher. Stir until frozen yogurt is melted. Stir in seltzer water, rum extract and coconut extract, if desired. Garnish with mint sprigs.

*Makes 12 ($\frac{1}{2}$-cup) servings*

# Pomegranate Green Tea Punch

3 cups boiling water
6 LIPTON® Green Tea Bags
2 tablespoons sugar
1 cup chilled pomegranate juice or cranberry juice cocktail

In teapot, pour boiling water over Lipton Green Tea Bags; cover and brew 1½ minutes. Remove Tea Bags; stir in sugar and cool.

In large pitcher, combine tea and pomegranate juice. Chill, if desired, or serve in ice-filled glasses.           *Makes 4 (8-ounce) servings*

# Strawberry-Apricot Punch

2 packages (10 ounces each) frozen sliced strawberries in syrup, thawed
2 cans (5½ ounces each) apricot or peach nectar
¼ cup lemon juice
2 tablespoons honey
1 bottle (2 liters) lemon-lime soda
Lemon slices or fresh strawberry halves (optional)

1. Place strawberries with syrup in food processor or blender; process until smooth.

2. Pour puréed strawberries into large punch bowl. Stir in apricot nectar, lemon juice and honey; blend well.

3. To serve, stir soda into strawberry mixture. Garnish with lemon slices.
*Makes 12 servings*

# Herbal Cranberry Punch

2½ cups cranberry juice cocktail
2½ cups water
  4 orange, apple or raspberry herbal tea bags
  2 to 3 tablespoons sugar (optional)

1. Combine cranberry juice and water in medium saucepan. Bring to a boil over medium heat. Add tea bags, remove from heat; cover. Let steep at least 5 minutes.

2. Remove tea bags and discard. Add sugar, if desired.

*Makes 6 servings*

# Celebration Punch

  1 can (46 fluid ounces) DEL MONTE® Pineapple Juice, chilled
  1 can (46 fluid ounces) apricot nectar, chilled
  1 cup orange juice
¼ cup fresh lime juice
  2 tablespoons grenadine
  1 cup rum (optional)
  Ice cubes

1. Combine all ingredients in punch bowl.

2. Garnish with pineapple wedges and lime slices, if desired.

*Makes 16 (6-ounce) servings*

# Dazzling
*desserts*

# Orange-Glazed Cocoa Bundt Cake

$^3/_4$ cup (1$^1/_2$ sticks) butter or margarine, softened
1$^2/_3$ cups sugar
  2 eggs
  1 teaspoon vanilla extract
$^3/_4$ cup sour cream
  2 cups all-purpose flour
$^2/_3$ cup HERSHEY'S Cocoa
$^1/_2$ teaspoon salt
  2 teaspoons baking soda
  1 cup buttermilk or sour milk*
    Orange Glaze (recipe follows)

*To sour milk: Use 1 tablespoon white vinegar plus milk to equal 1 cup.*

1. Heat oven to 350°F. Grease and flour 12-cup fluted tube pan.

2. Beat butter, sugar, eggs and vanilla in large bowl until light and fluffy; stir in sour cream. Stir together flour, cocoa and salt. Stir baking soda into buttermilk in medium bowl; add alternately with dry ingredients to butter mixture. Beat 2 minutes on medium speed. Pour batter into prepared pan.

3. Bake 50 minutes or until wooden pick inserted into center comes out clean. Cool in pan 10 minutes. Remove from pan to wire rack. Cool completely. Glaze with Orange Glaze; garnish as desired.

*Makes 12 to 14 servings*

Orange Glaze: Combine 2 cups powdered sugar, $^1/_4$ cup ($^1/_2$ stick) melted butter or margarine, 3 tablespoons orange juice, 1 teaspoon vanilla extract and $^1/_2$ teaspoon freshly grated orange peel in medium bowl; beat until smooth. Makes 1 cup glaze.

Variation: To make a vanilla glaze instead of the orange glaze, substitute 3 tablespoons water for orange juice and omit orange peel.

# Chewy Peanut Butter Brownies

3/4 cup (1 1/2 sticks) butter, melted
3/4 cup creamy peanut butter
1 3/4 cups sugar
2 teaspoons vanilla
4 eggs, lightly beaten
1 1/4 cups all-purpose flour
1/2 teaspoon baking powder
1/4 teaspoon salt
1/4 cup unsweetened cocoa powder

1. Preheat oven to 350°F. Grease 13×9-inch baking pan.

2. Beat butter and peanut butter in large bowl with electric mixer at low speed 3 minutes or until well blended. Add sugar and vanilla; beat until blended. Add eggs; beat until well blended. Stir in flour, baking powder and salt just until blended. Reserve 1 3/4 cups batter. Stir cocoa into remaining batter.

3. Spread cocoa batter evenly in prepared pan. Top with reserved batter. Bake 30 minutes or until edges begin to pull away from sides of pan. Cool completely in pan on wire rack. *Makes 3 dozen brownies*

# Chocolate Almond Cheesecake

Almond Crumb Crust (recipe follows)
3 packages (8 ounces each) cream cheese, softened
1¼ cups sugar
½ cup sour cream
⅓ cup HERSHEY₅S Cocoa
2 tablespoons all-purpose flour
3 eggs
2 teaspoons almond extract
1 teaspoon vanilla extract
Almond Whipped Cream (recipe follows)
Sliced almonds (optional)

1. Prepare Almond Crumb Crust.

2. Increase oven temperature to 425°F. Combine cream cheese, sugar, sour cream, cocoa and flour in large bowl; beat with electric mixer on medium speed until smooth. Add eggs, almond extract and vanilla; beat well. Pour into prepared crust.

3. Bake 10 minutes. Reduce oven temperature to 250°F; continue baking 55 minutes or until center appears set. Remove from oven to wire rack. Loosen cake from side of pan. Cool completely; remove side of pan.

4. Refrigerate several hours before serving. Garnish with Almond Whipped Cream and sliced almonds, if desired. *Makes 10 to 12 servings*

Almond Crumb Crust: Heat oven to 350°F. Combine ¾ cup vanilla wafer crumbs, ½ cup ground blanched almonds and 3 tablespoons sugar in small bowl. Stir in 3 tablespoons melted butter. Press mixture firmly onto bottom and ½ inch up side of 9-inch springform pan. Bake 8 to 10 minutes; cool.

Almond Whipped Cream: Combine ½ cup cold whipping cream, 2 tablespoons powdered sugar, ¼ teaspoon vanilla and ⅛ teaspoon almond extract in small bowl; beat until stiff. Makes 1 cup.

# Fortune Cookies

**12 paper fortunes**
   **Nonstick cooking spray**
 **2 egg whites**
**$1/3$ cup flour**
**$1/3$ cup sugar**
 **1 tablespoon water**
**$1/4$ teaspoon vanilla**

1. Write or type 12 individual fortunes or words of wisdom onto paper. Cut into $2^{1}/_{2} \times {}^{3}/_{4}$-inch strips.

2. Preheat oven to 400°F. Spray cookie sheet with cooking spray.

3. Whisk egg whites with wire whisk in small bowl until foamy. Add flour, sugar, water and vanilla; whisk until smooth.

4. Working in batches of 2, place 2 teaspoons batter on prepared cookie sheet; spread batter evenly with back of spoon to 3-inch round. Spray with cooking spray. Repeat. Bake 4 minutes or until edges are golden brown.

5. Remove cookies quickly from cookie sheet and invert onto work surface. Place fortune in center. Fold cookie in half, pressing on seam. Fold in half again, pressing to hold together. Cool completely. Repeat with remaining batter, re-spraying cooled cookie sheets with cooking spray after each batch.                                 *Makes 1 dozen cookies*

# Simply Special Brownies

 $^1/_2$ cup (1 stick) butter or margarine

 1 package (4 ounces) HERSHEY᠄S SPECIAL DARK™ Premium
   Chocolate Baking Bar, broken into pieces

 2 eggs

 1 teaspoon vanilla extract

 $^3/_4$ teaspoon powdered instant coffee

 $^2/_3$ cup sugar

 $^1/_2$ cup all-purpose flour

 $^1/_4$ teaspoon baking soda

 $^1/_4$ teaspoon salt

 $^1/_2$ cup coarsely chopped nuts (optional)

1. Heat oven to 350°F. Grease 9-inch square baking pan.

2. Place butter and chocolate in medium microwave-safe bowl. Microwave at HIGH (100%) 1 minute; stir. If necessary, microwave an additional 15 seconds at a time, stirring after each heating, until chocolate is melted and mixture is smooth when stirred. Add eggs, vanilla and instant coffee, stirring until well blended. Stir in sugar, flour, baking soda and salt; blend completely. Stir in nuts, if desired. Spread batter in prepared pan.

3. Bake 25 to 30 minutes or until wooden pick inserted in center comes out almost clean. Cool completely in pan on wire rack. Cut into bars.

*Makes 20 brownies*

# Sweetie Pies

½ cup (1 stick) butter or margarine, softened
1 (3-ounce) package cream cheese, softened
1 tablespoon granulated sugar
1⅓ cups all-purpose flour
½ cup finely chopped pecans
1 (21-ounce) can cherry pie filling
1 teaspoon almond extract

Put butter, cream cheese and sugar in a large mixing bowl. Beat with an electric mixer on medium speed 3 to 4 minutes or until smooth. Add flour and pecans; mix well. Roll dough into 1-inch balls. Press balls evenly onto the bottom and up the sides of 1¾×1-inch miniature muffin cups.

Combine cherry pie filling and almond extract. Spoon about 1 tablespoon cherry mixture into each pastry-lined cup.

Bake in a preheated 350°F oven 20 to 25 minutes, or until light brown. Let cool in pans 5 minutes. Transfer to wire racks to cool completely.

*Makes 2 dozen*

Favorite recipe from **Cherry Marketing Institute**

# Greek Date-Nut Swirls

1 cup *each* firmly packed dried figs and firmly packed pitted dates
1 cup coarsely chopped walnuts
$\frac{1}{2}$ cup water
$\frac{3}{4}$ cup granulated sugar, divided
1$\frac{3}{4}$ cups all-purpose flour
2 teaspoons ground anise seeds
$\frac{1}{4}$ teaspoon *each* salt, baking powder and baking soda
$\frac{1}{2}$ cup (1 stick) unsalted butter, softened
4 ounces cream cheese, softened
1 egg yolk
1 teaspoon vanilla

1. Combine figs, dates, walnuts, water and 3 tablespoons sugar in food processor or blender. Process until mixture is smooth.

2. Combine flour, anise, salt, baking powder and baking soda in medium bowl; set aside.

3. Beat butter, cream cheese and 3 tablespoons sugar with electric mixer at medium speed until creamy. Add egg yolk, vanilla and flour mixture; beat until soft dough forms. Form dough into ball; wrap in plastic wrap. Refrigerate 2 hours or until firm.

4. Place large sheet of waxed paper on smooth, dry surface. Roll dough into 13×10-inch rectangle with floured rolling pin. Gently spread fig mixture in even layer over dough. Beginning on one long side, lift waxed paper to roll up dough jelly-roll fashion. Spread remaining 6 tablespoons sugar on another sheet of waxed paper; roll log in sugar. Wrap sugared log in plastic wrap; refrigerate 4 hours or until firm.

5. Preheat oven to 350°F. Line two cookie sheets with parchment paper. Cut log into $\frac{1}{3}$-inch-thick slices (about 36 slices). Place 2 inches apart on prepared cookie sheets. Bake 12 to 14 minutes or until cookies are golden brown. Cool 1 minute on cookie sheets. Remove to wire racks; cool completely. Store in airtight container.    *Makes about 3 dozen cookies*

# Brandy Snaps with Lemon Ricotta Cream

**Cookies**

$\frac{1}{2}$ **cup (1 stick) butter**

$\frac{1}{2}$ **cup sugar**

$\frac{1}{3}$ **cup light corn syrup**

1 **cup all-purpose flour**

1 **tablespoon brandy or cognac**

**Filling**

$\frac{1}{2}$ **cup (1 stick) butter, softened**

$\frac{1}{2}$ **cup ricotta cheese**

$\frac{1}{4}$ **cup sugar**

2 **teaspoons grated lemon peel**

1 **tablespoon lemon juice**

1. Preheat oven to 325°F. For cookies, place $\frac{1}{2}$ cup butter, $\frac{1}{2}$ cup sugar and corn syrup in medium saucepan over medium heat; cook and stir until butter is melted and mixture is blended. Stir in flour and brandy.

2. Drop level tablespoonfuls of batter about 3 inches apart onto ungreased cookie sheets, spacing to fit 4 cookies per sheet. Bake one cookie sheet at a time about 12 minutes or until golden brown.

3. Cool cookies 1 minute. Remove each cookie from cookie sheet and quickly wrap around wooden spoon handle.

4. For filling, process $\frac{1}{2}$ cup butter, ricotta, $\frac{1}{4}$ cup sugar, lemon peel and lemon juice in food processor or blender until smooth.

5. Place filling in pastry bag fitted with plain or star tip, or in 1-quart resealable food storage bag with small corner cut off. Fill cookies just before serving.

*Makes 2 dozen cookies*

Dazzling Desserts

# Chocolate Banana Split Cake

1 sheet (18×12 inches) nonstick foil
1 cup packed brown sugar
$\frac{1}{2}$ cup (1 stick) unsalted butter, softened
2 eggs
2 very ripe bananas, mashed
1 cup all-purpose flour
5 tablespoons unsweetened cocoa powder
$\frac{3}{4}$ teaspoon baking soda
$\frac{1}{4}$ teaspoon salt
  Chocolate syrup
2 firm bananas, quartered
  Whipped cream or whipped topping
1 pint strawberries, sliced
  Chopped nuts

1. Preheat oven to 350°F. Line 9×5×3-inch loaf pan with foil, leaving 1-inch overhang on sides and 5-inch overhand on ends.

2. Beat brown sugar and butter in large bowl with electric mixer at medium speed until light and fluffy. Add eggs; beat until smooth. Add mashed bananas; beat until blended.

3. Combine flour, cocoa, baking soda and salt in medium bowl. Gradually add dry ingredients to banana mixture, beating until smooth.

4. Pour batter into prepared pan. Fold foil over batter to cover batter completely; crimp foil, leaving head space for cake to rise.

5. Bake 1 hour and 15 minutes or until toothpick inserted into center comes out clean. Cool 10 minutes on wire rack. Open foil and lift cake from pan. Cool completely.

6. Slice cake into 8 slices. Top with chocolate syrup, quartered bananas, whipped cream, strawberries and nuts. *Makes 8 servings*

# Cheery Apple-Cherry Twists

2 packages (8 ounces) cream cheese, softened
1 cup (2 sticks) plus 2 tablespoons unsalted butter, softened
$\frac{1}{4}$ cup plus $\frac{1}{3}$ cup granulated sugar
$\frac{1}{4}$ teaspoon salt
2 cups sifted all-purpose flour
4 Granny Smith apples, cored, seeded and chopped
$\frac{1}{2}$ cup dried cherries
$\frac{1}{4}$ cup whipping cream
2 tablespoons brandy
1 tablespoon lemon juice
1 teaspoon ground cinnamon
$\frac{1}{4}$ teaspoon ground cardamom
$\frac{1}{2}$ teaspoon ground ginger
Powdered sugar

1. Beat cream cheese and 1 cup butter in large bowl with electric mixer at medium speed until blended. Beat in $\frac{1}{4}$ cup sugar and salt. Beat in flour at low speed. Divide dough into 4 portions; wrap in plastic wrap. Refrigerate 3 to 4 hours.

2. Meanwhile, combine apples, cherries, remaining $\frac{1}{3}$ cup sugar, whipping cream, remaining 2 tablespoons butter, brandy, lemon juice and spices in large saucepan. Cook over medium heat until mixture comes to a boil. Reduce heat; stir and simmer 10 to 15 minutes or until thick and most juices are absorbed. Remove from heat. Cool completely.

3. Preheat oven to 350°F. Line cookie sheets with parchment paper. Process apple mixture in blender until chopped (do not purée). Roll dough disks into 10×4-inch rectangles on floured surface. Cut each rectangle into 7 (4×1$\frac{1}{2}$-inch) strips. Place 1 tablespoon filling lengthwise down center of strips. Lift dough ends; completely twist to form tube shape. Place 1 inch apart on prepared cookie sheets. Reroll any dough scraps.

4. Bake, one pan at a time, 22 to 26 minutes or until lightly browned. Cool completely. Sprinkle with powdered sugar. *Makes 28 twists*

# Layers of Mint Chocolate Grasshopper Pie

1⅓ cups (8-ounce package) YORK® Mini Peppermint Patties, divided
5 tablespoons milk, divided
1 packaged chocolate crumb crust (6 ounces)
1½ cups miniature marshmallows
1 tub (8 ounces) frozen whipped topping, thawed and divided
Additional sweetened whipped cream or whipped topping (optional)

1. Place ⅓ cup peppermint patties and 1 tablespoon milk in microwave-safe bowl. Microwave 30 seconds at HIGH (100%); stir. If necessary, microwave an additional 15 seconds at a time, stirring after each heating, until chips are melted and mixture is smooth when stirred. Spread on bottom of crust. Refrigerate while preparing next step.

2. Place marshmallows, ⅔ cup peppermint patties and remaining 4 tablespoons milk in small saucepan. Cook over medium heat, stirring constantly, until marshmallows are melted and mixture is well blended. Transfer to separate large bowl; cool completely.

3. Stir 2 cups whipped topping into cooled marshmallow mixture; spread over chocolate in crust. Set aside about 2 tablespoons peppermint patties; coarsely chop the remaining patties. Stir chopped pieces into remaining whipped topping. Spread over surface of pie.

4. Cover; freeze several hours or until firm. Garnish with remaining peppermint patties and additional whipped topping, if desired. Cover; freeze remaining pie.                    *Makes 6 to 8 servings*

Dazzling Desserts

# Creamy Lemon Cake

2 cups cake flour

2 teaspoons baking powder

$^1/_4$ teaspoon salt

1 cup granulated sugar

$^2/_3$ cup (1$^1/_3$ sticks) unsalted butter, softened

4 egg whites, at room temperature

$^3/_4$ cup buttermilk, at room temperature

1 teaspoon vanilla

1$^1/_4$ cups whipping cream

$^1/_2$ cup powdered sugar

1$^1/_2$ teaspoons grated lemon peel

$^3/_4$ cup prepared lemon curd

Sugared Rose Petals (recipe follows, optional)

1. Prepare Sugared Rose Petals, if desired.

2. Preheat oven to 350°F. Grease two 8-inch round cake pans. Sift flour, baking powder and salt into small bowl; set aside.

3. Beat sugar and butter in large bowl with electric mixer at medium speed until creamy. Beat in egg whites. Increase speed to high; beat 2 minutes. Reduce speed to low; add flour mixture alternately with buttermilk. Beat in vanilla until blended.

4. Divide batter between prepared pans. Bake 23 to 25 minutes or until toothpick inserted into centers comes out clean. Cool in pans on wire racks 15 minutes. Remove from pans; cool completely.

5. Meanwhile, whip cream until thickened. Add powdered sugar and lemon peel; beat until stiff peaks form. Refrigerate until ready to use.

6. Spread lemon curd evenly between 2 cake layers. Frost top and sides of cake with whipped cream mixture; refrigerate until set. Garnish with Sugared Rose Petals. *Makes 8 servings*

Sugared Rose Petals: Brush edible rose petals with 1 pasteurized egg white. Sprinkle generously with granulated sugar; set on wire rack to dry.

# Celebration Chocolate Mini Cupcakes

$^3/_4$ **cup all-purpose flour**
$^1/_2$ **cup sugar**
 **2 tablespoons HERSHEY⋅S Cocoa**
$^1/_2$ **teaspoon baking soda**
$^1/_4$ **teaspoon salt**
$^1/_2$ **cup water**
 **3 tablespoons vegetable oil**
**1$^1/_2$ teaspoons white vinegar**
$^1/_2$ **teaspoon vanilla extract**
    **Celebration Chocolate Frosting (recipe follows)**

1. Heat oven to 350°F. Line 28 small (1$^3/_4$-inch) muffin cups with paper or foil bake cups.*

2. Stir together flour, sugar, cocoa, baking soda and salt in medium bowl. Add water, oil, vinegar and vanilla; beat with whisk or mixer on medium speed until well blended. Fill muffin cups two-thirds full with batter.

3. Bake 11 to 13 minutes or until wooden pick inserted in center comes out clean. Remove from pan to wire rack. Cool completely. Frost with Celebration Chocolate Frosting. Garnish as desired.

*Makes 28 cupcakes*

*Batter can be baked in 8 standard (2$^1/_2$-inch) paper-lined muffin cups. Bake at 350°F for 20 to 25 minutes.*

## Celebration Chocolate Frosting

 **1 cup powdered sugar**
 **3 tablespoons HERSHEY⋅S Cocoa**
 **3 tablespoons butter or margarine, softened**
 **2 tablespoons water or milk**
$^1/_2$ **teaspoon vanilla extract**

Stir together powdered sugar and cocoa. Beat butter and $\frac{1}{2}$ cup cocoa mixture in medium bowl until blended. Add remaining cocoa mixture, water and vanilla; beat to spreading consistency. *Makes about 1 cup*

# Hot Chocolate Cookies

$\frac{1}{2}$ **cup (1 stick) butter, softened**
$\frac{1}{2}$ **cup sugar**
$\frac{1}{4}$ **teaspoon salt**
 **1 cup milk chocolate chips, melted, divided**
 **1 cup all-purpose flour**
   **Mini marshmallows, cut into small pieces**

1. Preheat oven to 350°F. Lightly grease cookie sheets or line with parchment paper.

2. Beat butter, sugar and salt in large bowl with electric mixer at medium speed until well blended. Add $\frac{1}{4}$ cup melted chocolate; beat until well blended. Gradually add flour, beating after each addition.

3. Shape dough by level tablespoonfuls into balls. (If dough is too soft, refrigerate 1 hour or until firm enough to handle.) Place 2 inches apart on prepared cookie sheets; flatten to $\frac{1}{2}$-inch thickness. Bake 15 to 17 minutes or until firm. Cool on cookie sheets 5 minutes. Remove to wire racks; cool completely.

4. Spread about 1 teaspoon remaining melted chocolate onto each cookie. Sprinkle with marshmallow pieces; press gently into chocolate. Refrigerate at least 1 hour or until set. *Makes about 2 dozen cookies*

**Chocolate Dipped Cherries (recipe follows)**
$2/3$ **cup plus 1 tablespoon sugar, divided**
$3/4$ **cup ($1^1/2$ sticks) butter or margarine**
$1/2$ **cup HERSHEY'S Cocoa**
$1/4$ **cup whipping cream**
$1^1/2$ **teaspoons vanilla extract**
$1/4$ **cup all-purpose flour**
 **2 eggs**
 **2 egg yolks**
$1/3$ **cup maraschino cherries, finely chopped**
 **Sweetened whipped cream (optional)**

1. Prepare Chocolate Dipped Cherries.

2. Heat oven to 400°F. Grease six 6-ounce custard cups. Sprinkle insides evenly with 1 tablespoon sugar. Place dishes in 13×9×2-inch baking pan. Melt butter in medium saucepan. Remove from heat. Whisk in cocoa, $1/3$ cup sugar, whipping cream and vanilla. Whisk in flour just until combined.

3. Beat eggs, egg yolks and remaining $1/3$ cup sugar in large bowl with electric mixer on high speed about 5 minutes. Beat in chocolate mixture on medium speed. Pour about $1/4$ cup into each prepared custard cup. Sprinkle evenly with chopped cherries. Pour remaining chocolate mixture into each cup.

4. Bake 13 to 15 minutes or until top of each cake looks dry. Let stand in cups 3 minutes. Loosen sides; invert onto serving plates. Serve warm with whipped cream and Chocolate Dipped Cherries.    *Makes 6 servings*

Chocolate Dipped Cherries: Drain 6 maraschino cherries with stems. Pat dry with paper towels. Place $1/4$ cup HERSHEY'S Semi-Sweet Chocolate Chips and $1/2$ teaspoon shortening (do not use butter, margarine, spread or oil) in small microwave-safe bowl. Microwave at HIGH (100%) for 45 seconds. Stir until chips are melted. Dip cherries into chocolate mixture. Place on wax paper-lined tray. Refrigerate until serving time.

# Cranberry Pound Cake

1 cup (2 sticks) unsalted butter
1½ cups sugar
¼ teaspoon salt
¼ teaspoon ground mace
4 eggs
2 cups cake flour
1 cup chopped fresh or frozen cranberries

1. Preheat oven to 350°F. Grease and flour 9×5-inch loaf pan.

2. Beat butter, sugar, salt and mace in large bowl with electric mixer at medium speed until light and fluffy. Beat in eggs, one at a time, until well blended. Reduce speed to low; add flour, ½ cup at a time, scraping down bowl occasionally. Fold in cranberries.

3. Spoon batter into prepared pan. Bake 60 to 70 minutes or until toothpick inserted into center comes out clean. Cool in pan on wire rack 5 minutes. Run knife around edges of pan to loosen cake; cool additional 30 minutes. Remove from pan; cool completely on wire rack.     *Makes 12 servings*

If you don't have fresh or frozen cranberries on hand, you can use dried sweetened cranberries. Simply cover 1 cup dried sweetened cranberries with hot water and let stand 10 minutes. Drain well before using.

# Jo's Moist and Delicious Chocolate Cake

2 cups all-purpose flour
1 cup granulated sugar
¼ cup unsweetened cocoa powder
1½ teaspoons baking powder
1½ teaspoons baking soda
1 cup mayonnaise
1 cup hot coffee
2 teaspoons vanilla
Powdered sugar (optional)

1. Preheat oven to 350°F. Grease and flour 10-inch bundt pan.

2. Sift together flour, sugar, cocoa, baking powder and baking soda in large bowl. Stir in mayonnaise, coffee and vanilla until batter is smooth. Pour into prepared pan.

3. Bake 30 minutes or until toothpick inserted near center comes out clean. Cool in pan on wire rack 10 to 15 minutes. Remove from pan; cool completely. Sprinkle with powdered sugar, if desired.

*Makes 12 servings*

# Sage Cake with Strawberries

$2/3$ cup milk, divided

14 whole fresh sage leaves, divided

4 egg yolks

1 teaspoon vanilla

2 cups cake flour, sifted

1 cup granulated sugar

1 tablespoon baking powder

$1/2$ teaspoon salt

$1/2$ cup (1 stick) butter, softened

Fresh strawberries, sliced

1. Preheat oven to 350°F. Grease and flour 9-inch cake pan.

2. Place milk in microwavable bowl. Tear 6 sage leaves in half; add to milk. Microwave on HIGH 2 minutes or until hot. Set aside to steep 15 minutes. Refrigerate mixture until cold. Strain through fine-mesh strainer.

3. Combine $1/3$ cup milk, egg yolks and vanilla in small bowl. Combine cake flour, sugar, baking powder and salt in medium bowl. Beat butter into flour mixture with electric mixer at low speed. Add remaining $1/3$ cup milk until ingredients are moistened. Gradually beat egg mixture into flour mixture on low speed. Increase speed to medium and beat 1 minute until light and fluffy.

4. Pour batter into prepared pan and arrange remaining sage leaves on top of batter. Bake 28 to 30 minutes or until cake is lightly golden. Cool on wire rack 10 minutes. Invert onto serving platter. Garnish with strawberries.

*Makes 12 servings*

# Intense Mint-Chocolate Brownies

1$\frac{1}{2}$ cups (3 sticks) butter, softened, divided
4 squares (1 ounce each) unsweetened chocolate
1$\frac{1}{2}$ cups granulated sugar
3 eggs
1$\frac{1}{2}$ teaspoons mint extract, divided
$\frac{1}{2}$ teaspoon salt
$\frac{1}{2}$ teaspoon vanilla
$\frac{3}{4}$ cup all-purpose flour
2 to 3 drops green food coloring
2 cups powdered sugar
2 to 3 tablespoons milk
$\frac{1}{3}$ cup semisweet chocolate chips

1. Preheat oven to 325°F. Grease and flour 9-inch square baking pan.

2. Melt 1 cup butter and unsweetened chocolate in top of double boiler over simmering water. Beat chocolate mixture, granulated sugar, eggs, $\frac{1}{2}$ teaspoon mint extract, salt and vanilla in large bowl with electric mixer at medium speed until well blended. Stir in flour. Spread batter in prepared pan. Bake 35 minutes or until top is firm and edges begin to pull away from sides of pan. Cool completely in pan on wire rack.

3. Meanwhile, beat 6 tablespoons butter, remaining 1 teaspoon mint extract and food coloring in large bowl with electric mixer at medium speed until fluffy. Add powdered sugar, $\frac{1}{2}$ cup at a time, beating well after each addition. Beat in milk, 1 tablespoon at a time, until frosting is spreading consistency. Spread over cooled brownies.

4. Place chocolate chips and remaining 2 tablespoons butter in microwavable bowl. Microwave on LOW (30%) 1 minute; stir. Repeat until chocolate is melted and mixture is smooth. Drizzle glaze over frosting; let stand 30 minutes or until set. Cut into bars. *Makes 2 dozen brownies*

# Lemon Drops

**2 cups all-purpose flour**
**$\frac{1}{8}$ teaspoon salt**
**1 cup (2 sticks) butter, softened**
**1 cup powdered sugar, divided**
**2 teaspoons lemon juice**
   **Grated peel of 1 large lemon (about $1\frac{1}{2}$ teaspoons)**

1. Preheat oven to 300°F.

2. Combine flour and salt in medium bowl. Beat butter and $\frac{3}{4}$ cup powdered sugar in large bowl with electric mixer at medium speed until fluffy. Beat in lemon peel and juice until well blended. Add flour mixture, $\frac{1}{2}$ cup at a time, beating just until blended.

3. Shape dough by rounded teaspoonfuls into balls. Place 1 inch apart on ungreased cookie sheets. Bake 20 to 25 minutes or until cookies are lightly browned on bottom. Cool 5 minutes on cookie sheets; transfer to wire racks to cool completely. Sprinkle with remaining $\frac{1}{4}$ cup powdered sugar.

*Makes about 6 dozen cookies*

# Black Bottom Cupcakes

1 package (8 ounces) cream cheese, softened
4 eggs
$\frac{1}{3}$ cup plus $\frac{1}{2}$ cup granulated sugar, divided
2 cups all-purpose flour
1 cup packed brown sugar
$\frac{3}{4}$ cup unsweetened cocoa powder
1 teaspoon baking powder
$\frac{1}{2}$ teaspoon baking soda
$\frac{1}{2}$ teaspoon salt
1 cup buttermilk
$\frac{1}{2}$ cup vegetable oil
$1\frac{1}{2}$ teaspoons vanilla

1. Preheat oven to 350°F. Line 20 standard ($2\frac{1}{2}$-inch) muffin cups with paper or foil baking cups. Beat cream cheese, 1 egg and $\frac{1}{3}$ cup granulated sugar in small bowl until smooth and creamy; set aside.

2. Combine flour, brown sugar, cocoa, remaining $\frac{1}{2}$ cup granulated sugar, baking powder, baking soda and salt in large bowl; mix well. Beat buttermilk, remaining 3 eggs, oil and vanilla in medium bowl until well blended. Add buttermilk mixture to flour mixture; beat about 2 minutes or until well blended.

3. Spoon batter into muffin cups, filling about three-fourths full. Spoon heaping tablespoon cream cheese mixture over batter in each cup; gently swirl with tip of knife to marbleize.

4. Bake 20 to 25 minutes or until toothpick inserted into centers comes out clean. Cool cupcakes in pans on wire racks 5 minutes. Remove from pans; cool completely. *Makes 20 cupcakes*

# Cheesecake 5 Ways

**Crumb Crust (recipe follows)**
**3 packages (8 ounces each) cream cheese, softened**
**$3/4$ cup sugar**
**3 eggs**
**1 teaspoon vanilla extract**

1. Prepare Crumb Crust. Heat oven to 350°F.

2. Beat cream cheese and sugar in large bowl until smooth. Add eggs, one at a time, beating well after each addition. Stir in vanilla. Pour into prepared crust.

3. Bake 45 to 50 minutes or until almost set.* Remove from oven to wire rack. With knife, loosen cake from side of pan. Cool completely; remove side of pan.

4. Cover; refrigerate several hours or until chilled. Just before serving, garnish as desired. Cover and refrigerate leftover cheesecake.

*Makes 10 to 12 servings*

*Cheesecakes are less likely to crack if baked in a water bath.*

Crumb Crust: Heat oven to 350°F. Stir together 1 cup graham cracker crumbs and 2 tablespoons sugar in small bowl; blend in $1/4$ cup ($1/2$ stick) melted butter or margarine, mixing well. Press mixture onto bottom and $1/2$ inch up side of 9-inch springform pan. Bake 8 to 10 minutes. Cool.

Chocolate Cheesecake: Increase sugar to $1 1/4$ cups and add $1/3$ cup HERSHEY'S Cocoa. Increase vanilla extract to $1 1/2$ teaspoons.

Toffee Bits Cheesecake: Prepare cheesecake as directed. Stir $1 1/3$ cups (8-ounce package) HEATH® BITS 'O BRICKLE® Toffee Bits into batter.

Chocolate Chip Cheesecake: Prepare cheesecake as directed. Stir 1 to $1 1/2$ cups HERSHEY'S MINI CHIPS™ Semi-Sweet Chocolate Chips into batter.

Mocha Cheesecake: Prepare Chocolate Cheesecake, using HERSHEY'S SPECIAL DARK™ Cocoa. Add 1½ teaspoons instant coffee granules to batter.

Mocha Toffee with Chocolate Chips Cheesecake: Prepare Mocha Cheesecake as directed. Stir ¾ cup HEATH® BITS 'O BRICKLE® Toffee Bits and ¾ cup HERSHEY'S MINI CHIPS™ Semi-Sweet Chocolate Chips into batter.

## Stars and Stripes Cupcakes

**42 cupcakes, any flavor**
**2 containers (16 ounces each) vanilla frosting**
**Fresh blueberries, washed and dried**
**Fresh strawberries, washed, dried, stemmed and halved**

1. Frost cupcakes with vanilla frosting.

2. Sprinkle 9 cupcakes with blueberries. Decorate remaining cupcakes with strawberry halves.

3. Arrange cupcakes to form United States flag.          *Makes 42 cupcakes*

# Cherry-Almond Clafouti

½ cup slivered almonds, toasted*
½ cup powdered sugar
⅔ cup flour
⅔ cup granulated sugar
¼ teaspoon salt
½ cup (1 stick) butter, cut into pieces
⅔ cup milk
2 eggs
½ teaspoon vanilla
1 cup fresh cherries, pitted and quartered

*To toast almonds, spread in single layer on baking sheet. Bake in preheated 350°F oven 8 to 10 minutes or until golden brown, stirring frequently.

1. Preheat oven to 350°F. Spray 4 (6-ounce) ramekins with nonstick cooking spray; place on baking sheet.

2. Process almonds in food processor or blender until coarsely ground. Add powdered sugar; pulse until well blended. Add flour, granulated sugar and salt. Pulse until well blended. Gradually add butter, pulsing just until blended.

3. Combine milk, eggs and vanilla in small bowl. With food processor running, gradually add milk mixture to almond mixture. Process until blended. Remove blade from food processor; stir in cherries.

4. Divide batter among prepared ramekins. Bake about 50 minutes or until tops and sides are puffy and golden. Let cool 5 to 10 minutes.

*Makes 4 servings*

Note: Clafouti is a traditional French dessert made by layering a sweet batter over fresh fruit. The result is a rich dessert with a cake-like topping and a pudding-like center.

# Perfectly Peppermint Brownies

$^3/_4$ cup **HERSHEY:S Cocoa**

$^1/_2$ **teaspoon baking soda**

$^2/_3$ **cup (1$^1/_3$ sticks) butter or margarine, melted and divided**

$^1/_2$ **cup boiling water**

2 **cups sugar**

2 **eggs**

1$^1/_3$ **cups all-purpose flour**

1 **teaspoon vanilla extract**

$^1/_4$ **teaspoon salt**

1$^1/_3$ **cups (8-ounce package) YORK® Mini Peppermint Patties**

1. Heat oven to 350°F. Grease 13×9×2-inch baking pan.

2. Stir together cocoa and baking soda in large bowl; stir in $^1/_3$ cup butter. Add boiling water; stir until mixture thickens. Stir in sugar, eggs and remaining $^1/_3$ cup butter; stir until smooth. Add flour, vanilla and salt; blend completely. Stir in peppermint patties. Spread in prepared pan.

3. Bake 35 to 40 minutes or until brownies begin to pull away from sides of pan. Cool completely in pan on wire rack. Cut into bars.

*Makes about 3 dozen brownies*

# Acknowledgments

***The publisher would like to thank the companies and organizations listed below for the use of their recipes and photographs in this publication.***

ACH Food Companies, Inc.

Birds Eye Foods

California Tomato Commission

Cherry Marketing Institute

Delmarva Poultry Industry, Inc.

Del Monte Corporation

Dole Food Company, Inc.

Florida Department of Agriculture and Consumer Services,
Bureau of Seafood and Aquaculture

Florida Department of Citrus

The Hershey Company

Kahlúa® Liqueur

Lee Kum Kee (USA) Inc.

Mott's® is a registered trademark of Mott's, LLP

National Cattlemen's Beef Association on behalf of The Beef Checkoff

National Honey Board

Newman's Own, Inc.®

North Carolina SweetPotato Commission

Ortega®, A Division of B&G Foods, Inc.

Reckitt Benckiser Inc.

Sargento® Foods Inc.

Reprinted with permission of Sunkist Growers, Inc. All Rights Reserved.

Unilever

Veg•All®

# METRIC CONVERSION CHART

## VOLUME MEASUREMENTS (dry)

$1/8$ teaspoon = 0.5 mL
$1/4$ teaspoon = 1 mL
$1/2$ teaspoon = 2 mL
$3/4$ teaspoon = 4 mL
1 teaspoon = 5 mL
1 tablespoon = 15 mL
2 tablespoons = 30 mL
$1/4$ cup = 60 mL
$1/3$ cup = 75 mL
$1/2$ cup = 125 mL
$2/3$ cup = 150 mL
$3/4$ cup = 175 mL
1 cup = 250 mL
2 cups = 1 pint = 500 mL
3 cups = 750 mL
4 cups = 1 quart = 1 L

## VOLUME MEASUREMENTS (fluid)

1 fluid ounce (2 tablespoons) = 30 mL
4 fluid ounces ($1/2$ cup) = 125 mL
8 fluid ounces (1 cup) = 250 mL
12 fluid ounces ($1 1/2$ cups) = 375 mL
16 fluid ounces (2 cups) = 500 mL

## WEIGHTS (mass)

$1/2$ ounce = 15 g
1 ounce = 30 g
3 ounces = 90 g
4 ounces = 120 g
8 ounces = 225 g
10 ounces = 285 g
12 ounces = 360 g
16 ounces = 1 pound = 450 g

## DIMENSIONS

$1/16$ inch = 2 mm
$1/8$ inch = 3 mm
$1/4$ inch = 6 mm
$1/2$ inch = 1.5 cm
$3/4$ inch = 2 cm
1 inch = 2.5 cm

## OVEN TEMPERATURES

250°F = 120°C
275°F = 140°C
300°F = 150°C
325°F = 160°C
350°F = 180°C
375°F = 190°C
400°F = 200°C
425°F = 220°C
450°F = 230°C

## BAKING PAN SIZES

| Utensil | Size in Inches/Quarts | Metric Volume | Size in Centimeters |
|---|---|---|---|
| Baking or Cake Pan (square or rectangular) | $8 \times 8 \times 2$ | 2 L | $20 \times 20 \times 5$ |
| | $9 \times 9 \times 2$ | 2.5 L | $23 \times 23 \times 5$ |
| | $12 \times 8 \times 2$ | 3 L | $30 \times 20 \times 5$ |
| | $13 \times 9 \times 2$ | 3.5 L | $33 \times 23 \times 5$ |
| Loaf Pan | $8 \times 4 \times 3$ | 1.5 L | $20 \times 10 \times 7$ |
| | $9 \times 5 \times 3$ | 2 L | $23 \times 13 \times 7$ |
| Round Layer Cake Pan | $8 \times 1 1/2$ | 1.2 L | $20 \times 4$ |
| | $9 \times 1 1/2$ | 1.5 L | $23 \times 4$ |
| Pie Plate | $8 \times 1 1/4$ | 750 mL | $20 \times 3$ |
| | $9 \times 1 1/4$ | 1 L | $23 \times 3$ |
| Baking Dish or Casserole | 1 quart | 1 L | — |
| | $1 1/2$ quart | 1.5 L | — |
| | 2 quart | 2 L | — |